WHAT THE FUZZ? is the most unexpect... ... ...
in a long, long time. Heartfelt and hilarious, this memoir charts
the maturity of its author, from a bumbling kid utterly lacking
in self-confidence, into an unexpected American blue-collar
superhero. This book is chockful of magical moments,
moments of levity, and moments of love, friendship, and
decency. I read this memoir in a single-sitting and can't wait
for more of Ruefman's quirky, kind-hearted
writing. WHAT THE FUZZ? is a literary underdog that I'll be
rooting and cheering for long into the future.

-- NICKOLAS BUTLER, bestselling
author of SHOTGUN LOVESONGS
and GODSPEED

In *What the Fuzz*, Daniel Ruefman gives an uproarious glimpse
behind the mask, with stories both hilarious and humbling. He
shows us that oftentimes, the mascot is the hardest working
person in the stadium.

-- JOE NIESE, author of HANDY
ANDY: THE ANDY PAFKO
STORY and BURLEIGH GRIMES:
BASEBALL'S LAST LEGAL
SPITBALLER

If you like mascots, you'll fall in love with Shooter and C. Wolf.
Shooter (hockey) throws himself down stairs for cheap cheers,
while C. Wolf (baseball) faces near-death experiences--both
real and imagined. Behind both furry faces is the author
himself, who brings his story to life with humanity and heart.
This is for those who like their stories warm and fuzzy.

—David Aretha, award-winning
author of MALALA YOUSAFZAI
AND THE GIRLS OF PAKISTAN

WHAT THE FUZZ?

SURVIVAL STORIES OF A MINOR

LEAGUE MASCOT

To You —

The Reader. I Hope you Enjoy
these memories.

WHAT THE FUZZ?
Survival Stories of a Minor League Mascot

With Gratitude & Friendship —

by

DANIEL RUEFMAN

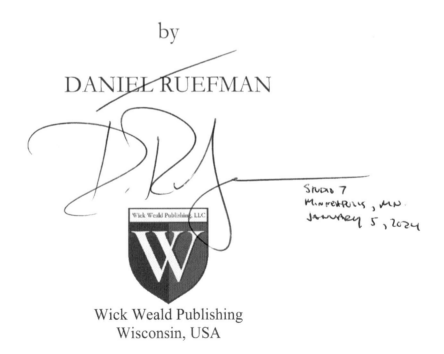

Studio 7
Minneapolis, MN.
January 5, 2024

Wick Weald Publishing
Wisconsin, USA

Library of Congress Cataloguing-in-Publication Data
Registration Number: TXu 2-305-590
Names: Ruefman, Daniel, author
Title: What the Fuzz? Survival Stories of a Minor League Mascot | by
Daniel Ruefman
Description: First Edition. | Hudson, WI: Wick Weald Publishing, LLC,
[2022]

Identifiers: ISBN: 978-1-7352697-7-1 (paperback)
                    ISBN: 978-1-7352697-3-3 (hardback)
                    ISBN: 978-1-7352697-6-4 (eBook)

Subjects: Memoir—Sports | Memoir—Humor

10 9 8 7 6 5 4 3 2 1
First Edition

Disclaimer: The following is a work of creative nonfiction that celebrates
the formative experiences of the author. Although the events detailed are
true to the author's memory, some names and identifying traits of
individuals depicted have been changed to protect their privacy.

For my wife who married me despite it all.

For my children who might know me a bit better because of it.

And for my dad, who always showed up with the insurance

cards.

Contents

What Will You Do for Work?
(én Español)

"How the heck did you get a job as a mascot in professional baseball?"

That mildly annoying question has been echoed by fans, friends, and family long after my brief career in the Minor Leagues ended in 2006. In truth, it's not the question that I've found so frustrating, nor the tones of bewilderment, revulsion, or pity that often accompany it. What has bothered me so much is the fact that, after all these years, I don't have a better answer for it. Ask me, "Hey, how'd you manage to get a job as a mascot in professional sports?" and the honest response is simple—I have no idea.

However, if you pressed me further on this issue, I might have told you the story of how a weekend job at Chuck E. Cheese led to an unlikely opportunity. I might have described how that opportunity led to a mafia-style job offer in a dark parking lot after a game. But if you asked me about the first moment that the idea of becoming a mascot entered my mind, I'd probably trace that back to a paragraph that I wrote in jest for a Spanish class at Fort LeBoeuf High School in Waterford, Pennsylvania back in the Spring of 2000.

It was my third class with Senorita Clutter. We had just moved beyond advanced verb conjugations and syntax and were about to embark on the most difficult assignment to date—a written paragraph. We were then required to read these paragraphs in front of the class and have them displayed publicly for the entire school to read. The assignment was not unlike the one we had been asked to complete a hundred times in elementary school. I suppose that's fitting, given my reading level in Spanish at that point was somewhere between pre-kindergarten and fledgling first grader.

Senorita Clutter was a thin, athletic woman, who taught spinning classes at a local fitness and racquet club. She had a collection of knickknacks, figurines, toys, and stuffed animals that she had acquired over the years while traveling the Spanish speaking world. Having studied originally in Spain, she spoke the language with a perfect Castilian dialect. Her European lisp softened her words as she presented the class with her assignment prompt.

"What will you do for work?" she asked.

She searched the room, starting with a student in the back corner farthest from me. The student answered, and she proceeded methodically, row by row, posing the question for each student in turn, then whirled to write the appropriate words on the whiteboard behind her. I raked my memory for the things that stood out to me as a child. Police officer? Teacher? One of those diggers on *Jurassic Park*? But as I zeroed in on each of those ideas, I heard one of my classmates answer—*policía, profesor, arqueólogo*. No sooner had I thought "writer" when a jerk named Jason leapt from his seat and boldly said *"escritor"* with far more enthusiasm than was necessary.

Senorita Clutter's eyes roved over the class, slipping up and down the rows, and one by one she bid us each to speak. I was seated in the last row, but she was moving quickly, and I began to panic.

She soon called on a kid named David whose parents owned a drive-up ice cream shop at the edge of town. Fresh back from his family's annual Caribbean cruise, he elaborated more on his answer than anyone in class up until that point. He explained, in perfect Spanish, that he was just going to go into the family business, running the store, selling ice cream and Coney dogs in the summer. I glowered at him, irritated both by his proficiency with the Spanish language and with his apparent ready-made career. Then it struck me. If he was just going to do what his parents did, couldn't I? Could this assignment be that easy? Maybe the answer was as simple as telling the class what my dad did. No problem; I just needed to figure out exactly what that was.

I didn't fully understand the full scope of my father's business at that time. His career seemed to have layers. He worked for a company where he bent sheet metal into surgical sinks, mortuary refrigerators, autopsy tables, and something called a "cadaver-go-round"—a sort of combination lazy Susan-dumbwaiter for dead people. Throughout my childhood, he and I would go "bumming around town" and on these occasions we would show up at the shop where he worked. When I was really young, he'd buy me chips from the vending machine and I ate as he wrapped up a bit of innocuous paperwork. When he was done, he would take me on a tour of the place on an old forklift—but only when nobody else was there. In hindsight, I suspect that would probably qualify as an

OSHA violation of some type, but for five-year old me, it was a great way to spend a Saturday. As I got older, the forklift rides were traded for tutorials, during which my father showed me how to make some of the stranger products they manufactured.

Sitting there in Spanish class, watching Senorita Clutter drawing closer, I thought of what my dad had shown me just that prior weekend. He had taken me into a super-heated corner of the shop that was tucked behind long plastic strip curtains, spattered with dried foam insulation. He pulled out a series of steel molds, smeared on some sort of industrial lubricant, then showed me how to use the valve at the end of a hose to inject the chemicals into the steel molds. We worked a full day on these and produced a stack of large foam boxes.

"What are these for anyway?" I remember asking, as I built the cardboard boxes that would ultimately be used to ship the foam ones.

Dad peered over the wire frames of his glasses. The t-shirt he was wearing was already flecked with dry foam from the week before and his thinning hairline glistened with sweat.

"Skin," he answered coolly and without pause, as if this was the most reasonable thing in the world.

"What?" I gave my head a little shake. I couldn't have heard that right.

"They're for human skin. For transplant."

The horror must have shown on my face because he went on to a very detailed explanation of biology and medical technologies that I found more than a little confusing at the time. Finally, he tried his best to spell it out for me.

"Say you got burned in a fire," he said. "The doctors might need to graft the skin from an organ donor onto you to help save your life. Now what if the donor is in Pittsburgh, but you need the skin in Cleveland? That's where these boxes come in." He gave one of the boxes a thump on the lid. "The doctors will put the donor skin into these boxes and send it on a helicopter to Cleveland. The skin must stay at a certain temperature in order to be viable for transplant, and these foam boxes keep the skin at that temperature so that it doesn't go bad before they are grafted onto the person who needs them. Understand?"

I did not. At this stage of my life, I was not what you would call "a thinker." But I nodded just the same.

Sitting in Spanish class, I broke his explanation down into the most fundamental parts. It seemed simple enough, on the surface. Maybe I could write my Spanish paragraph about that?

I rifled through my Spanish to English dictionary, for each of the words, and wrote down the sentence, "*Quiero hacer cajas para la piel humana.*" Simple. Roughly translated, I had just written down, "I want to make boxes for human skin."

It was at that moment that I realized that some people might consider my dad's job a little creepy. As I re-translated those words, my mind immediately flitted to the film *Silence of the Lambs*—that scene where Buffalo Bill was dancing naked in front of a camera while wearing the dead scalp and skin that he harvested from his victims. It was an image that made me realize that reading that sentence aloud would probably destroy all hope that I would ever have for a normal social life.

I wasn't particularly popular in high school. Then again, I wasn't entirely unpopular either. I fell somewhere in the middle, eccentric enough to endear myself to teachers and keep the number of my friends down to a manageable minimum. Still, I was close enough to "normal" that I could generally find a date to school dances if I really wanted.

However, with this one sentence, I was teetering on the edge of social suicide. All I needed to do was say aloud those words that I had written in my notebook and declare for the entire class that what I most dreamed of doing in my life was making giant boxes that had no tangible purpose other than holding and storing human skin.

No. That's the kind of thing that'll get you an appointment with the guidance counselor, and possibly a permanent spot on the no-fly list.

I scribbled out that sentence and refocused my attention to the subject of jobs. Unique—not creepy—jobs. There had to be something. Something out of the ordinary. Something that no other student would pick. Senorita Clutter shuffled closer. And then, it struck me. Over her shoulder, I saw a strange, green stuffed animal sitting on her filing cabinet in the corner of the classroom. The sheen of its fake fur shone in the light of the overhead fluorescents. It triggered something. The creature was familiar. I focused on the fur, and then another image rose to the forefront of my mind like a messianic vision. It was a large bird, lime green, and covered with that same fur. A giant parrot!

A few summers before, my dad had taken my sister and me to our first Major League Baseball game to watch the Cardinals take on the Pirates at Three Rivers Stadium. It was the year or so after Mark McGwire broke the single-season home run record, and they had already announced plans to tear down the stadium so that the franchise could move to their new home at PNC Park. My dad thought that was as good a time as any to make the trip, to show us the stadium that his father had taken him to as a kid. He wanted to share that memory with us before the stands were reduced to a riverside parking lot that would serve the new ballpark. I remember filing up the concrete stairs when the song "Surfin' Bird" boomed from the stadium speakers and, to a chorus of cheers, a giant neon green parrot streaked across the infield below. He strutted about the warning track, smacking the palm of his oversized baseball glove, joining a few of the players for a quick game of catch during pregame warmups.

As quickly as the memory came, it was pushed aside by the sensation of Senorita Clutter's eyes clamping onto me.

"*Benji?*" she called me by my Spanish name, *"Y tu?"*

"Un momento, por favor," I said.

I retrieved, again, my Spanish to English dictionary and leafed through as quickly as I could. Finally, I fingered the page that I was looking for and answered her gaze with three words.

"Mascota de profesional," I said, offering what I had hoped would be an innocent smile.

"Mascota?" Senorita Clutter asked, somewhat accusatorily. Then, thinking I must have had the wrong word, the corners of her lips curled into a smile. *"En Inglés?"*

"I would like to be a professional mascot," I said confidently.

My classmates chortled around me and I watched Senorita Clutter's jaw slacken slightly. Her eyebrows drew up and she blinked her wide, blue-gray eyes at me. The laughter continued, directed more at her expression of befuddled amusement than at my absurd career choice. But hey, at least this choice was better than "maker of skin boxes," right?

That night, I sat on my old twin bed, scribbling my paragraph on a piece of loose-leaf notebook paper. When I finished, I cut it out and pasted the words onto the piece of colored construction paper. I drew a few pictures—a baseball, a glove, and a bat. Then, wanting to add just a touch of flair, I remembered the baseball cards that I had hoarded as a child.

They were on the shelves inside my closet. Hidden among them were several specialty cards that depicted the team mascots of every Major League franchise, and among them was the Pittsburgh Pirates' Parrot.

Perfect.

I dug through the collection and pulled that card from the plastic sleeve that held it. I took a small piece of Scotch Tape, folded it over, and used it to affix the card to the construction paper so that the surprised parrot appeared to be reading my words, dancing in celebration of my stated career goal.

When the time came for us to share our writing with the class, I read my paragraph aloud and then pinned it to the display wall outside Senorita Clutter's classroom. Ultimately, I claimed an "A" on the assignment and then moved on without giving any additional thought to the matter.

After all, it was just a joke. Right?

Unexpected Invitation

You should always be careful with humor. Sometimes when we say or do something in jest, the universe makes note of it. Regardless of your intent in the moment, jokes from the past have this inevitable way of jumping up and biting you when you least expect it. When that happens, you have two choices: you can lean into it, or you can run away from it.

Three years had passed since Senorita Clutter's Spanish class and I hadn't spared a single thought about the paragraph that I wrote in high school. The strange thing was that, all these years later, I was no closer to having an answer to that very basic question.

In the summer of 2002, just before I began my second year of college at Edinboro University, I found myself slumped in the corner of the costume closet at our local Chuck E. Cheese. Enveloped by darkness and the fake floral aroma of air fresheners and chemical cleaners, I was exhausted. The antiseptic scent made me want to puke, but at least it was quiet in there. Through the thick door, I could barely hear the clatter and clang of skeeball machines and the screams of children mobbing the prize counter at the height of their sugar rushes. Like a giant, sweat-soaked ragdoll, I slumped against the wall opposite the door, trying to just enjoy the next five minutes before I'd need to go back out there. Throughout the day, the opportunities to just sit in silence were extraordinarily rare and I learned to make the most of those moments as they came.

A knock at the door indicated the end of this break. It was the signal that the party was ready for me.

Last one, I thought.

I stood, retrieved the fuzzy fiberglass face from the floor beside me, and heaved it up over my head. Inside, the foam pads of the hockey-style helmet squished against my forehead, sending a full day's worth of cold sweat pouring down my face, burning my eyes. I blinked and blew air toward my eyebrows, until the worst of the sweat stopped running. Soon, my eyes adjusted to the burning and my field of vision (for the most part) began to clear. My heart thudded against my ribs and I drew a deep breath, then pushed my way out into the light.

The return of the deafening sound caused my head to throb with a renewed vigor, and before the costume closet door was closed, two kids were already wrestling with my knees. They tugged and twisted at the baggy pantlegs, taxing the Velcro that kept them tethered to the fat suit that gave Chuck E. Cheese his iconic shape in the early 2000s.

That sort of greeting was inevitable. I came to expect it every time I stepped in the suit, but no matter how much I anticipated it, I was rarely ready for it. The kids threw their weight against me with such force that I staggered, barely able to keep myself from crumpling to the ground on top of them.

"All right, girls, all right," Jenny said. "Chuck has a birthday party to go see, but he'll be out to play after, okay?"

Jenny was a wiry brunette who had been working as a party hostess for the past three years while earning her degree in early childhood education. She stooped and handed each of the kids a few tokens, then sent them off giggling in the direction of the game room. When she drew up again, she shot me a conciliatory smirk and took me by a fuzzy, four-fingered paw.

"Let's go, Chuck," Jenny continued. "There's someone you have to meet."

She led me past the prize counter and we threaded ourselves through the line of guests at the registers. We passed the salad and beverage bars and eventually arrived at the entrance of the showroom. Around the perimeter were several booths where families could sit and eat while watching the animatronic band blink and click as a video played on the flat-screen television on the stage. The music that they allegedly played, boomed through the inhouse sound system. There were four long rows of tables at the center of the room. This is where the birthday parties were held. Each one was capable of accommodating twenty children, but only the row nearest the door was occupied a that time. The tables there were covered with plastic table cloths, half-eaten pizza, party plates, and cups.

Jenny let go of my paw and I hovered behind the half wall, just outside the showroom. After all, it was her job to warm up the real stars of the birthday show.

"All right, everyone," I heard her say. "Are you guys ready for Chuck E.?"

"Yeah!" all of the little voices shouted in unison.

"It's a busy day, though, and I think he's having a hard time finding your party," Jenny said. "But I bet if you called his name real loud, he'd hear you. Let's call him together. Ready? Chuck E.! Chuck E.!"

Without missing a beat, the kids joined in, clapping with each syllable.

"Chuck E.! Chuck E.! Chuck E.!"

"I'm not sure he can hear you," Jenny said.

The chanting doubled in volume. I played a game of peek-a-boo through the entryway of the showroom, ducking in and out of view, as one or two of the kids went wild.

"There he is!" they shouted.

"Where?" Jenny asked.

"Behind you!"

Jenny looked around with an exaggerated look of confusion and shrugged.

"I don't see him."

"There! There! At the door!"

I tiptoed up behind Jenny then, motioning for everyone to be quiet, but when she turned, I leapt up in surprise and shook my giant head in silent embarrassment. The partygoers cheered, leaping up and greeting me with a hurricane of hugs.

Jenny used this opportunity to sneak beside the stage and open a door where the party supplies and sound system were stowed.

"You ready, Chuck?"

I flashed a thumbs-up and Jenny reached up and pushed in the VHS tape that said "Birthday Show 2002." The speakers crackled overhead as the tape loaded. The robotic mouse, monster, bird, dog, and chef whirred and clicked, as they turned and blinked at random intervals. When the music started, I made my way to the front of the stage, and the kids returned to their seats at the party table.

Jenny and I started to teach the kids the dance moves for this particular song as the VHS tape instructions boomed from the speakers. That's when I looked up and saw that *he* was still there.

On a riser near the rear of the room, a man in his mid-twenties leaned back in one of the booths. He stared at the party with an odd little smile. He had been there for most of the afternoon watching us, occasionally snapping a covert photo of the party with his Nokia flip phone. I wouldn't say that his presence was particularly threatening. He was a tall guy with brown, Abercrombie hair. He wore a hooded sweatshirt and jeans and might have passed for a college student. But if he had been shorter, older, and without those disarming dimples, I might have described his behavior as borderline creepy.

After the first song, the show paused. Jenny and I ducked into the kitchen to grab the cake. I pulled off Chuck's head and leaned against the stainless-steel sink while Jenny pulled a chocolate birthday cake from the walk-in cooler and poked a few candles into the half-frozen frosting.

"Hey, have you noticed that guy in the back of the showroom?"

"Who?" Jenny asked, a little distracted.

"That guy at the booth," I said. "The one who has just been sitting by himself there for the last two or three parties."

"Oh," she said thoughtfully. "Yeah. I think he knew one of the parents from my three o'clock party."

"Yeah, but they left, didn't they?"

"A while ago, yeah," Jenny said. "So?"

"So, why is he still here?"

Jenny shrugged. "It's a free country, isn't it? Maybe he just likes our pizza."

I wrinkled my nose and grimaced. "Unlikely."

Jenny chuckled at that, then unconcerned, she scooped up the cake and turned to leave the kitchen. I pulled on the giant head and followed.

After dancing the corporate jig to the "Bake, bake, baking a cake" devil song, Jenny lit up the candles and the birthday girl, who was sitting at the head of the table, made her wish. When the show was done, Jenny tossed in the VHS labeled "Summertime" and the animatronic band on stage resumed their job as a peripheral source of entertainment. For a while, I hung back in the showroom for some photos. Every now and again, I'd glance toward the back of the room. He was still there. Every time I looked up, he was there, his wide, enthusiastic eyes dominating an otherwise placid grin. It was as if he were a recruiter with a cult, eyeing his newest initiate. Whoever that guy was, he was starting to make me feel uneasy.

Once done with the party obligations, I shuffled around the restaurant, played a few games with the kids, spread some free tickets around the crowd, and tracked down those two girls who had ambushed me outside the costume room, to keep the promise that Jenny had made to them before the party. Finally, forty-five minutes after I had emerged, I ducked back into the costume room for the last time that day.

I took my time there, basking in the relative silence as I wiped down Chuck E.'s fiberglass head and helmet. I sprayed his baggy clothes with a double dose of Febreze and hung them on the hooks to dry, and just before I stepped out, I gave the room a quick spritz with that nauseating faux-floral air freshener. Turning off the light, I peeked out first to ensure that no kids were around, then slipped out as stealthily as I could. The problem was, I wasn't stealthy enough. As I checked the door handle to ensure that the room was locked behind me, a heavy hand gripped my shoulder. Startled, I whipped around. It was the man who had spent most of the afternoon sitting in the back of the showroom.

He was even taller than he had appeared when he was folded into that booth. Well over six feet tall, he grinned down at me with a too-white smile, flashing every single one of his impossibly straight teeth.

"Hey—I'm Brent," the man said.

Good for you, I thought, though I bit my tongue.

"I'm the marketing director with the Erie Otters."

In an instant my creeped out suspicion was replaced with confusion. I knew a bit about the Otters. They were a major junior hockey team in the Ontario Hockey League. They were one of just two American teams playing in the league at that time and were fresh off their first OHL Championship. After that, their regional fanbase exploded, as several of their players were promptly recruited during the subsequent NHL draft. I was never much of a hockey fan. As a matter of fact the only hockey games I had ever watched up until that point were in some cheesy Emilio Estevez movie.

Brent extended me a business card. Embossed with dark blue writing was the name Brent Smith, Marketing Director. Beside his name was the image of an otter wearing an oversized hockey helmet and brandishing a taped stick directly above the rather lazy logo for the OHL.

"Okay," I said, uncertain of where this conversation was about to go.

"You were the one in the suit, right?" Brent asked. Then without waiting for an answer, he continued. "Great job. You've got a lot of talent."

"Oh," I said. "Thanks?"

"Been doing it long?" he continued with a bubbly enthusiasm usually reserved for winners of the Publisher's Clearing House or a game of Cow Pie Bingo at the Waterford Fairgrounds.

"Not too long."

"Wow, great. Really great. Do you like it?"

I wasn't entirely sure that he was really listening to me. I brushed passed him, hoping that by rushing my return to work he might decide to simply move along. Instead, Brent did the opposite. He turned and followed.

"I mean, it sure looks like you enjoy it."

"Eh," I shrugged. "It's a paycheck. I suppose it can be fun, though."

I retrieved a bottle of cleaner and some blue paper towels from the cabinet under the beverage bar and began wiping the deposits of sticky syrup from the stainless-steel surface. This wasn't strictly my responsibility, but if I acted busy enough, I was still hopeful that he'd get the hint. He didn't.

"Well, did you ever think of taking it to the next level?"

Next level? What the hell was he talking about? There were no levels. I was working a minimum wage job, slinging pizzas, and dressing up like a giant mouse for tips at birthday parties. It wasn't even *entry* level. It wasn't on the scale. The suggestion otherwise seemed nonsensical to me at the time.

"Next level?" I finally asked. "What do you mean?"

"Well, no sense in beating around the bush," Brent said. "I can see you're busy. But we've been searching for a mascot for this upcoming season and haven't had too much luck. But I've been watching you today and I thought that I'd invite you to try out. Think you'd be interested in giving it a shot?"

This had to be a joke, right? I mean, who drops in at the local Chuck E. Cheese to scout for mascots? Then again, where *would* you go to scout for prospective mascots? I mean, it's not like they had job fairs for this sort of thing, but there had to be a system in place, right? Then it dawned on me. Brent hadn't been spying on kids' birthday parties all day. He was just spying on me. In that moment, I wasn't sure whether that detail made this situation more or less awkward.

"How about you think it over for a couple of days," Brent said. "If you'd like to give it a whirl, give me a call. Just let me know soon. The season's about to start and we need to figure something out."

I never thought that I would actually call him. No reasonable person would have taken this job offer seriously. A guy with a business card stalking you while you worked, then offering you a job? That's how horror movies start out. But I couldn't tell him that. Personal rejection is how horror movies often end for minor characters. So, I humored him.

"Alright," I said. "I'll think about it."

He shook my hand and left. I pocketed his card and returned to work with no real intention of dedicating any further thought to it. It was nearing the end of summer and my college classes would be resuming soon. I didn't need another job, really. The money here wasn't great, but the managers were willing to work around my class schedule and it was— safe. By that I mean the work itself was easy, my coworkers were pleasant, and I could generally pick up as many hours as I wanted during the winter months. It was stable and reliable. Why mess with any of that?

Then my mind flitted back to that paragraph in Spanish class. For the first time in three years, I remembered that moment when Senorita Clutter fixed her eyes on me and asked what I would do for work. I had no clue then and—if it was possible—I had even less of a clue now. But as I watched Brent leave, the answer I had given back then drifted to the forefront of my mind and the words *mascota de profesional* cut through everything else.

The words rose like a specter from my adolescence and for the first time, I gave the prospect serious consideration. I had taken the job at Chuck E. Cheese because the daycare center where I had been working closed. I was in a bind and a few friends from high school referred me to their general manager. Like most jobs for college students, I hadn't planned to work there. I just sort of fell into it. Call it a coincidence, but as Brent's offer hung in the air around me, it felt more akin to providence. The universe had opened up, selected the most asinine career prospect I had ever thought of and seemed to be saying, *hey, you asked for it, didn't you?*

The Otters were a big deal around town. Junior hockey or not, for a city the size of Erie, that team was the closest that many fans would ever get to seeing a pro hockey game. Then I imagined the thousands of fans who would occupy a sold-out arena downtown. With the chant from the birthday party fresh in my mind, I imagined what it would be like to stand in front of that crowd, to listen to ten thousand people cheering for me.

I suppose it would be fair to chalk it up to vanity, but even a faux popularity of that scale was intriguing to someone who had never experienced anything like it. The image lodged itself in my mind. Add that to Brent's flattery, singling me out for a job well done, and suddenly the idea didn't sound so ridiculous.

That night, the more I thought about it, the more I started to actually want the job. Still, I didn't want to get my hopes up. Brent said that there'd be a tryout and I figured that with such a unique opportunity that the competition would be fierce.

21

When I woke the next morning, I rolled over in bed, pulled my phone from its charger. I had left Brent's card on the nightstand beside it. I didn't want to waste any more time mulling things over. Now that I wanted it, I was convinced that the opportunity was bound to slip away.

I punched Brent's number into the keypad and he answered on the second ring.

"Hey, Brent? It's Dan. We met at Chuck E. Cheese yesterday?"

"Oh, hey. It's good to hear from you," he said and his enthusiasm radiated through the phone. "So have you given any more thought to being Shooter?"

Trying not to sound like I wanted the job too much, I tried to play it cooler than I felt. "What the hell," I said. "I'll give it a whirl."

First Night, First Ouch

Brent said "tryout." I distinctly heard that. So, imagine my surprise when he told me that the first time that I'd put on the suit was on the day of the home opener. Perhaps, the quality of my performance at Chuck E. Cheese was more than enough for Brent to persuade the team owners to hire me on for the season. Then again, more than likely, there were no other candidates for the job.

As the day of the home opener approached, I was rather excited. Until, that is, Brent called me with a specific request.

"We had this great idea," Brent began. "We want you to skate out onto the ice ahead of the team, waving a 'Let's Go Otters' flag.

Suddenly my nerves ticked up a bit.

It may sound odd, but even though I grew up in the Great Lakes region and had several friends who played youth hockey, I never really spent much time on the ice. By "not much time" I actually mean that never—not once—had I ever strapped on a pair of hockey skates as a kid. My parents usually claimed that ice skating, video games—basically anything kids found to be fun—was far too expensive for our modest means. Yet, here I was, nineteen years old, and my new employer was informing me that my first skate was to occur in a giant otter costume and in front of more than six thousand screaming hockey fans.

"Just skate around the rink a few times, wave that flag, and get everyone all fired up. It'll be great," Brent said.

Well, it looked easy enough and I was a reasonably good athlete at the time. How difficult could it be to learn how to skate in a few hours? So, I bought myself a used pair of skates from a secondhand sports store, showed up a few hours early at the Tulio arena, and once the Zamboni finished smoothing the surface, I stepped out onto the ice. It was a lot slicker than it looked from the stands. In places, the water seemed to bead on the ice like dew on a rainslicker.

After a few falls, and adjustments, I found my legs and acclimated to the surface. Sure, stopping was still a problem. Spoiler alert: It would always be a problem—but I was reasonably comfortable doing what I needed to do and was able to complete two quick laps while waving the flag without a major wipeout. Satisfied with that, I exited the ice without any significant problem. Unfortunately, all of this was without the added complication of a full costume, hockey pads, and giant head with virtually no visibility. Plus, the bulk of all that extra equipment would do nothing to help me balance on a steel edge that was just a few millimeters thick. If anything, the overall bulk would ultimately sabotage any effort I might make to stay on my feet, and afterward, I suspected that Brent probably knew that.

As I stepped off the ice, Brent nodded his approval. "That should do," he said. "Now you just have to meet Shooter."

He handed me the key to Shooter's locker room and led me into a honeycomb of hallways that stretched throughout the bowels of the Erie Civic Center. We passed the Otter's clubhouse, which housed a luxurious locker room worthy of an NHL team. At first, I thought Brent was about to lead me inside, but apparently access was so restricted that not even Shooter was permitted in there. We continued on through a large garage that housed four wheelers outfitted with snow plows and various machinery used to maintain the Minor League Baseball stadium next door. Finally, on the opposite side of the building, Brent led me down a damp, poorly-lit hallway.

The corridor contained a series of three or four small, poorly maintained locker rooms, which were occupied at that point by the team visiting from Kitchner, Ontario. Brent pushed past the visitors who were clamoring about the hallway. About half of them were in their practice gear, while others wore only boxer shorts and kicked a deflated soccer ball against the cinderblock walls with their bare feet. I flinched at the *bang* of the ball, which rang like a gunshot down the corridor. I thought that Brent was going to take me back to the front office, which also branched off of this area, but, sadly, no. Instead, he stopped at a small metal door smack dab in the middle of the chaos. On the opposite wall was a table with three five-gallon jugs of Gatorade on it. As it turned out, Shooter's dressing room was directly across from the away team's watering hole. It was like a meerkat digging a burrow inside the same den as dozens of ravenous hyenas.

"Here we are," Brent said, nodding toward the door and handing me the brass key at the end of an Otter's lanyard. "This one is you."

The ball banged again and the visiting team whooped in response. I fumbled the ancient key into the lock.

When the door swung open, the stink of mingled mildew and body odor hit me full in the face. My nostrils burned and eyes watered. The room was slightly larger than a janitor's closet. Along the wall to my right was a toilet, sink, and mirror. To my left was a small shower, its walls thick with black mold. Next to the shower was a small sitting area with two plastic school chairs and a shelf with a closet rod bolted beneath it. From that rod hung two matted suits of ragged, brown fur, some hockey pads, and a jersey with the name "Shooter" stitched across its shoulders. On the shelf above the jersey, next to a tattered duffle bag from the 1970s, sat the vacant stare and lopsided grin of the dismembered mascot.

"Everything you should need is in there," Brent said. "Keep the key with you. It's the only one we have, so don't lose it. Have a good game!"

With that, Brent was gone, without ever crossing the threshold. I'm sure game day was hectic for him, especially for the season opener, but there's a part of me that suspected that he knew what lay behind that door and thought it best—for his own health—not to venture too close to it.

As I slipped into the body suit for the first time, I noticed a funk that seemed to seep from the molecular structure of the thing. I was sure that it was recently laundered, but the aroma that clung to Shooter was much like summer laundry left to fester wet in the washing machine for three days. What was worse, the smell seemed to intensify as the uniform sopped up my own sweat. Once the fur suit, the hockey pads, jersey, gloves, and shoes were in place, I slipped on Shooter's head and found that it was impossible to see through the damn thing.

By design Shooter's giant blue eyes and toothy grin were made from the same mesh material that would theoretically allow me to see out into the world. However, the blue eyes were positioned over my forehead, making them impossible to see through. The mouth was positioned directly in front of my gaze, but it was smushed closed. One of the small plastic support columns that propped open Shooter's mouth was missing. I took the head off and tried to figure out how I could prop the mouth up so I could actually see something. It was then that I noticed, next to the toilet, was an almost empty toilet paper roll and that empty roll was almost as wide as Shooter's teeth were tall.

I popped the cardboard roll from the dispenser and propped it inside and was shocked when the cardboard carried the weight of the head. It was almost perfect. Proud of my own ingenuity, I tossed the head back on and swaggered out to greet the Otter's faithful for the first time.

***

The crowd filtered into their seats as shooting practice wrapped up, and the teams returned to their respective locker rooms. Once again, the Zamboni prepared the surface for the start of the game while I laced up my skates and took my place behind a curtain. The lights dimmed and I gathered up my flag. I checked the chin strap to ensure that my new head would remain on my shoulders at all times, no matter what happened out there. Afterall, the first rule of mascotting was never let the head come off in public.

The bells tolled and anticipation built to the haunting melody of an entrance theme worthy of the Undertaker in the WWE. Then my cue came. A guitar riff wailed across the ice and the murmuring crowd gave way to whoops and cheers. Two spotlights threaded figure eights, blue line to blue line, then swept the crowd. I stepped onto the ice with the flag in my hand and watched the lights come together on me—looking more like a rabid muskrat than a cute river otter. I felt a rush of adrenaline, followed by an urge to suddenly vomit. I'd have to fight that. Shooter smelled bad enough as it was, without introducing the contents of my stomach to the mix.

This is it, I thought to myself, and immediately I followed that thought with, *Don't fall, don't fall, don't fall. . .*

I kicked off the boards, bent forward, and for a few seconds the flag billowed magnificently overhead, displaying its message in the spotlights for the entire arena to see. Beneath it, my knees started buckling. I straightened up, regaining my balance for a heartbeat, but I was going too slow. The flag laid itself impotently against its pole. I needed more speed. I kicked against the ice again, trying desperately to get some momentum.

"Don't fall, don't fall, don't fall," I muttered to myself, attempting to lift my chin and peer out ahead of me. That was a mistake.

The head was a counterweight. When I lifted my chin, it tilted too far back. With one arm, I held the wooden flagpole while the other began windmilling. I leaned back and felt one foot leave the ice. Before I could whisper the word "shit," the cold hard surface rose to meet my back.

The force knocked the wind out of me. As I lay there, waiting for my lungs to expand again, I heard a thousand fans roaring with laughter, applause, and catcalls. Attempting in vain to force my lungs to fill, I glanced out of the corner of Shooter's meshed mouth. The team was directly behind me. One of the players, perhaps Chris Campoli or Cory Pecker—it's impossible to know for sure—skated by me and took up the team flag while his teammates, in an orderly procession, prodded me with their sticks as they skated a circle around their side of the arena.

The wet fur suit was sticky against the frozen surface. I pushed myself up, looked back, and I felt my face flush inside the overheated head. I had initially thought that my final kick had carried me close to center ice. I knew now that assumption was wrong. I had fallen less than ten feet from the door. Finally, I stood and wobble-skated like a toddler back to the gap in the boards and stepped off the ice. By the time I got there, the announcer was instructing the fans to stand for a singing of the Canadian and American national anthems. The player with the flag slid by, handed it to me, and joined his teammates along the blue line.

As I passed by the bleachers, a few kids held their hands out for a high-five, to which I grudgingly obliged, while a few of the older ones bopped Shooter's head and taunted me. There was some residual laughter, so I fixed my gaze on the floor ahead of me as I exited the arena through a black curtain.

Behind the curtain, on the landing of a stairwell outside the locker room, Brent was waiting by the table of snacks that the billet families (the host families with whom the players lived) stocked before every home game. Brent's face was split by a wide grin, and he appeared to be wiping a tear from his cheek. I took off the head and Brent laughed a little harder, shaking his own. He gestured toward a tray of cheese and crackers. Glad for the excuse, I removed my gloves and fixed myself a small plate, giving him time to regain his composure.

"Well," he chuckled, "that's not quite what I had in mind."

"Yeah—I'll do better next time."

"Good luck beating that."

He was clearly enjoying himself. If I didn't know any better, I'd say he was pleased to see me wipe out. I found this attitude a little unsettling.

"What do you mean?" I said through a mouthful of crackers. "I bombed."

He laughed a bit more vigorously at that.

"Yeah, you did!" Brent said. "But you have to remember, you're paid to entertain. To make the people laugh. Mission accomplished."

"Okay," I rolled my eyes. "But shouldn't a mascot be—you know—cool?"

"Sure, but if we can't have a *cool* mascot, the next best thing is a clown."

That comment hurt. Until then, my life of mediocrity had always been a challenge and had led to some major self-esteem issues. Being a clown, the brunt of everyone's jokes was not something that sounded very appealing. Brent adjusted his tact.

"Hey, just think of it this way," he said with a shift to seriousness. "It could have been worse."

"Oh, yeah? How's that?"

"You could have wiped out on Kitchner's side of the ice. Those kids are real jerks."

Three Gimmicks

Every celebrity has a trademark—that little dance move or gimmick that sets them apart. Michael Jackson had the moonwalk, Bo Jackson had his third-person catch phrase, and Redfoo had his stylish hornrims. Well, much like these public figures, there are many mascots vying for attention out there as well. Their success relies on their ability to stand out. The Pirate Parrot had his standing backflip, Clammy Sosa had his appetite for umpires and referees, and the Phillie Phanatic had his party-favor tongue and pelvic thrusts.

In any case, when I started working in the OHL, the pressure to perform was immediate. Brent made it clear that my grotesque parody of skating would take me only so far in this business.

"You have to make *this* Shooter special," Brent told me, handing me the dressing room key before the second game of the season. "It's your job to get people to sit up in their seats and say *WOW!* Understand?"

It seemed simple enough, so I nodded, accepted the key, and headed to my dressing room down the visiting team's corridor. There was still time before the game got started, and I was sure that I could think of something that would grab people's attention.

I slid into the unlaundered suit, still damp with sweat from the season opener. The moisture seemed to unlock the accumulated stench, a bouquet of smells that included traces of body odor from every human being who had ever donned that suit before me. To call it gross would have been an understatement, but I was a naïve college student and they were paying me. Though I never really got used to the smell, after a few minutes on the inside my eyes eventually stopped watering. So, I headed up to the main concourse and greeted the fans on their way through the turnstiles.

Preoccupied with posing for photos, signing autographs, and delivering high-fives, I nearly missed the team's curtain call. I ran back to my dressing room, grabbed my skates, and hustled into position with the team behind the curtain. By the time I was there, Brent was standing beside the door with the blue "Let's Go Otters!" flag. I sat down along the wall and tugged off my shoes and prepared to strap on my skates.

"Let's go without the skates tonight," he suggested.

"How come?" I asked. "I'm sure I'll do better tonight."

"Yeah," he said, adopting a professional demeanor that was unlike him. "It's kind of a liability thing. And since we pay you in cash, the owners want to figure out where you'd stand with worker's comp and stuff."

I shrugged, tossed my skates aside, and retied my shoes. The lights of the arena dimmed just as I finished the bow, and Brent handed me the flag and opened the door to the ice.

"All right, just walk on out there, wave the flag, and step to the side," he said. "Cuz these guys are coming right behind you."

The entrance was uneventful. I shuffled out onto the ice, the spotlight hit me, and when guitar riff sounded, the team exploded out of the door beside me. And how that crowd cheered. When the final player was on the ice, I shuffled away and the door slammed shut. Brent frowned at me as I picked up my discarded skates and exited through the black curtain to the billet room. I took off Shooter's head and attempted to get some fresh air.

"So, any good ideas for tonight?" Brent asked.

Ideas? Ideas for what? I hesitated. After slipping into the suit, I sort of forgot about our pregame conversation. It was only my second day and I was just getting acclimated to the arrangement. Still, I didn't want to disappoint.

"Oh, yeah," I lied. "I've got ideas."

"Cool," Brent said, looking a little more at ease. "I'll see you out there then."

My creativity was blocked. Until then, most of what I had done had been scripted by others. It was one thing doing a birthday dance that was semi-choreographed at the corporate headquarters of Chuck E. Cheese's. It was quite another thing to figure out the moves on my own.

I was just one game into my mascot career and I was already losing confidence in myself. After stomping on the steel stairs of the lower stands and leading the crowd for a third chant of *Let's Go Otters!* I could tell that the crowd was getting bored. Thinking that a bird's-eye view might help me to visualize something, I climbed one of the stairwells to the uppermost sections.

I sat on the stairs there and watched part of the game, surveying the arena for a source of inspiration. For several minutes, I stared at the ice, but nothing came.

In the next section over, a large group of college guys occupied a few rows. They were part of a fraternity at one of the local colleges and appeared to be celebrating something. A red-faced frat boy spotted me and waved me over. I had no other ideas, and no place to be just then, so I figured, why not pay them a visit.

I walked over and sat on the stairs next to the guy who waved me over. His rancid beer breath found its way inside, somehow managing to overpower Shooter's all-natural funk. He leaned over me, spilling some of his beer onto my jersey.

"Shooter," he began. "You know what'd get this crowd going?"

I looked around at the arena. There were fewer people today than there had been for the home opener, and rows across the aisle from where they were sitting were mostly empty. I turned back and shrugged.

"Dude," he said, "somersault down the stairs."

The idea, like his breath, reeked of stupidity. No rational human being would ever somersault intentionally down the stairs. The upper levels of the arena were constructed of poured concrete. Two-thirds of the way down, the concrete gave way to retractable metal risers. Neither of these materials were particularly forgiving. I turned back and raised an eyebrow. Then, realizing that he couldn't see me, I gave an exaggerated shrug and vigorously shook my head.

"Dude. Think about it." He thumped me twice between the shoulder blades. "You got pads, right?"

I cocked my head to the side, wondering where he was going with this.

"I'm tellin' you—it's totally safe. Plus..." He gave Shooter's head another thump and I felt the pillow-like head jostle around a bit. "...with this shit, you might as well be rolling down a hill in a ball of bubble wrap."

This guy was crazy. I shook him off and twirled my finger around Shooter's ear to communicate that point to him. The red-faced man chuckled and downed the remainder of his beer.

"Dude, I've seen other mascots do crazier things," he said. Before adding craftily, "The last Shooter would have done it."

The funny thing about being nineteen years old was that I had a good six years before I'd feel the effects of a fully functional, pre-frontal cortex. I know now that teenagers are inherently brain damaged, and in such a state, you're particularly susceptible to peer pressure.

I resisted the suggestion for another moment or two, but the strange thing was that the longer I sat there, the more I thought about what Brent had said about wowing the crowd. That thought led to the inevitable question: How would I do it?

In less than two minutes, this inebriated fan had gone from doofus to drunken Descartes. I slapped and squished Shooter's giant head, testing just how well the material and padding would absorb the shock.

"Don't overthink it," he said. "Just go for it."

I stomped on the concrete stairs, considering just how wide the space was between the safety railing in this section and seats. Leaning forward, I measured it with my shoulder pads. Shooter *would* fit.

"Come on," he goaded. Then he elbowed his buddy who sat next to him. Together, they started the chant. "Shoo-ter! Shoo-ter! Shoo-ter!"

The frat boys clapped on each syllable of Shooter's name and their words grew louder, enveloping the rest of the section. Then the next, and the next.

"Shoo-ter! Shoo-ter! Shoo-ter!"

The peer pressure intensified. People in the lower seats craned their necks to get a look at what I was about to do and, in that moment, I was actively considering it. The crowd carried the chant and soon the entire arena was united behind me.

There was a penalty on the ice, and as the referee blew the play dead, the red-faced man's hand found my back, thudding me on the shoulder pads again.

"It's easy, dude. Gravity," he said. "Just tuck and— ROLL!"

As he said it, he gave me a shove, and instead of fighting, I went with it. I tucked the oversized pillowed head between my knees and kicked off of the concrete stairs. One somersault turned into two—three—four—five! So far, so good. Six—seven—eight!

Then I panicked.

The pads seemed to be doing their job. I didn't feel a thing for most of the way down. The problem was that I was picking up speed and, just like my practice rounds on the ice at the home opener, I hadn't quite considered the whole stopping thing. The concrete stairs turned to steel and I knew I was almost to the bottom of the section. I couldn't see. Everything was spinning so much. Then out of the corner of Shooter's mesh-covered mouth, I caught a glimpse of the boards straight ahead of me. This time, when I felt my feet make contact with the stairs, I simply stood up. This action threw the full force of my body into the plexiglass.

BOOM!

I slammed against the boards that separated the ice from the crowd and the sound reverberated, shaking the plexiglass of the entire section. The boards wobbled and I fell back onto my haunches. Stunned by the collision and dizzy from the fall, I lay back on the stairs and I heard nothing. Nothing except the crowd. The whoops, the hollers, the cheers.

When I finally picked myself up, the fans in the seats on either side of the aisle grabbed at me, barked their approval, and shook my paws. And, just like the drunk college kid had predicted, everything was fine.

My heart pummeled my chest from the inside and my paws were shaking. So, I ducked back into the billet room, removed my head, and tried to calm myself with a few deep breaths. It didn't take long for Brent to find me there. The smile on his face was wider and brighter than the one he had worn when he introduced himself to me outside the costume closet at Chuck E. Cheese.

"Did you hear them?" he asked.

"Hear who?"

"Everybody!" he exclaimed. "That was awesome!"

I shrugged, trying to make sense of what happened. It was something I had no intention of doing, then—before I could think about it—it was done. It was rash, completely illogical, but in that moment, I was a little proud. It hadn't been my idea to tumble down the stairs, but I owned it after that. And odd as it might seem, while the team owners expressed liability concerns over my wiping out on the ice, they never raised a single objection to me somersaulting down a flight of stairs.

For weeks, I used that gimmick. Two to three times a game, when the referees stopped play, I popped up randomly in different areas of the arena and somersaulted—usually only on the lower half of the stands where the concrete gave way to retractable steel stairs and seating. It was quicker that way, enabling me to somersault, throw my body against the boards, and be done before play could resume. I also didn't have to contend with the sections of stairs that had been narrowed by the placement of hand railings. Over time, the more I somersaulted, the better I got at it. I was able to control the speed with which I flipped, able to pause in a headstand partway down, and then continue. I knew how many times I could flip on each aisle before I reached the plexiglass, and I usually timed it perfectly, delivering a louder bang with each attempt.

That is, until I got cocky.

One day, while I was playing around, I paused midroll and then lost count of how many somersaults I had completed.

Two? Three? Yes—three. Definitely three.

I continued on then, as I always did, tucking and rolling, careful to let Shooter's shoulder pads and head take the force of each flip. Finally, after the seventh, I went to kick my body into the boards. The only problem was that the boards weren't there. My legs shot straight out, and my lower back and hips connected with the sharp corner of the steel stairs. This single miscalculation cost me a sacral contusion and a recommendation from an ER physician to "try not to do anything stupid" for at least four to six weeks.

As most college students can understand, I couldn't afford to take that much time off. I simply had to adapt to the seemingly reasonable restriction of not throwing myself down the stairs for the amusement of others. I needed time to heal, but what could I do to wow the crowd now? With my trademark move out of the repertoire, I needed to come up with something else. I needed another gimmick.

***

Chuck-a-puck. Pretty much every hockey team in the country has this promotion. It was that time between two periods when they strategically place trash cans in various places on the ice and fans, for a few dollars, can purchase pucks and try to "chuck" them into the trashcans, for a chance to win fabulous prizes. Ours included coupons for a half-priced carwash, a free ticket to one of the Otters' undersold games, or a T-shirt signed by yours truly. Yes, indeed. Those prizes were almost worth the $5 price tag for participation.

After all the pucks were tossed, a few guys from Cycle City rode out on four-wheelers, outfitted with the latest in snowplow technology, and it was from them that I gained my next gimmick.

It all started a few weeks after my visit to the ER and the explicit orders from the physician on call to "try to not do anything stupid." I was in the garage at the east end of the arena where the chuck-a-puck cleanup crew was waiting for the end of the period. An intern was dragging the giant Rubbermaid trash bins out of the corner.

"So, what's wrong, Shooter?" one of the guys on the four-wheelers asked. He had a thick beard and wore a black Carhart coat over his Erie Otters hoodie. "Looks like you lost a little bounce in your step tonight."

"Got hurt," I said. "Something about a bruised sacrum."

"What the hell's a sacrum?"

"A bone, I said, turning my back to him and indicating an area right above Shooter's tail. "Somewhere around here. Doc says I have to take it easy for a while."

"Bummer," the guy said. "Shooter just hasn't been the same tonight."

I shrugged. The man's face furrowed and he considered me for a long moment.

"Hey, you know what'd be funny?" he asked. "If Shooter here would go out and plow up some of those pucks."

"I'm not sure about that," I said, glancing nervously at the massive machine he was perched upon. "Never really ridden one of those before, and without peripheral vision I'd be afraid of losing control and smashing into someone."

"No way," the man waved me off. "If my ten-year-old can drive this thing then you can."

I shook my head. "I don't think so."

"Don't you wuss out on us, Shooter," the man said. "I mean, these things drive themselves nowadays. All you really have to do is point it in the right direction."

"Sorry," I said, wondering how I'd control a massive ATV on the ice if I couldn't even be trusted with a pair of used hockey skates. "But I don't think I'd want to learn how to drive one of these things on the ice of an arena with so many people around. It could go badly."

"Well, what if we started you on something a little smaller," his partner chimed in. This guy was a little younger, clean shaven with a receding hairline. "Would you give it a try then?"

The guys on the four-wheelers exchanged a knowing look, but I didn't quite follow. Then deciding that it was best to leave the door open, I answered with a weak, "eh, we'll see."

The next game, as they unloaded the four-wheelers into the garage, there was an extra machine with them. It was tiny and red and looked as if it were made almost entirely of plastic.

"How about this one?" the man asked. "This one is so small and simple to operate. It's literally designed for children."

I sat on top of it and felt like a giant. I imagined what it would look like, having a giant otter riding around on something so compact. The image reminded me of the Shriner's Club in their little cars during parades. I always enjoyed them. And thus was born my next gimmick.

When the time came for the next chuck-a-puck, the civic center staff opened the massive door along the east wall, and the boards behind one of the goals folded open on their huge hinges. Two interns moved the goals to the side, and the plow team gave me the signal. I was to be the first one on the ice. I hit the ignition and the Lilliputian engine whined to life under me. Then, I squeezed the throttle. It was surprising just how much kick the machine had. It had only one gear, but I tore onto the ice faster than I would have thought possible. The transition from concrete floor to ice went practically unnoticed until, at center ice, I locked the brakes and turned the handlebars. The tiny four-wheeler spun withershins, until I came to a stop near the blue line on the far side of the arena. That was all it took for me to shed the last of my inhibitions.

Chuck-a-puck fast became my favorite part of every game. I spent several minutes zipping about the ice and fans took turns trying to hit me with pucks, instead of landing them into the prize barrels. That was fine with the front office. With each game the team sold more pucks, and interestingly enough, they had to pay out fewer prizes. That's what you call a win-win in the world of sports marketing.

For most of that season, I zipped around harder and faster, occasionally gunning it across the ice and smashing into the rink walls. Every now and again, I'd knock a fuel line or wire loose, and the four-wheeler would cut out. I'd push my ride back into the garage area, where the guys from Cycle City would carry out a quick repair, and before the next game, I'd be back on the ice crashing into the walls and prize buckets all over again. But, like Icarus, I grew drunk on my revelry. One day, I pushed too hard and flew too close to the sun.

As usual, when the garage door went up and the rink walls swung open, I tore out onto the ice. I spun donuts, locked the brakes, and slammed into the walls repeatedly. The chucked pucks rained down on me and I decided to go for one last donut on the blue line. Whether it was my own carelessness or the accumulation of pucks under my tires that was responsible, I suppose we'll never be sure. All I know is that something caught my wheel and as I leaned in to perform the stunt, I skidded off course, the engine cut out, and I rolled it. Shards of red plastic were scattered about, and before I could tell what had happened, I was on the ground, watching gasoline pour from a broken fuel line onto the ice.

The crowd cheered their approval and the crew from Cycle City carted the wreck off the ice. The Zamboni driver, a white-haired man in his sixties, studied the gasoline that had pooled along the wall. He chewed his tongue and shook his head while I stood and accepted my accolades. But when I walked off the ice, I ventured a last glance in his direction. He had begun chipping away at the ice where the gasoline contamination had occurred, scooping it into buckets.

As the guys from Cycle City cleared off the rest of the surface, the old Zamboni driver was joined by a handful of other civic center staff, chipping and shoveling all along the boards.

"Hey, nice goin', Shooter!" the guy in the Carhart jacket boomed when they returned the four-wheelers to the garage. "You killed it!"

I pulled off my head once the doors were closed and bent over the wreck. Most of the damage looked superficial— the plastic fenders mainly.

"Can't we fix it?"

"We could," he said, but it wouldn't be worth it. Probably take more for us to fix it than the thing is worth. I mean, new, this is just a couple of hundred bucks."

"Kind of a shame," I said. "It was a fun little ride."

"Yeah, looked it."

"So," I said, drawing myself up to full height. "When can I get a new one?"

The guy laughed as he climbed down from his own massive ride, crossing the floor, and leaning over my totaled quad. "You don't."

"Why not?"

"Two reasons. First, my boss didn't really know what we were doing with this one—and I'm not buying my kid *two* busted four-wheelers for his birthday. Second, you just gave every parent out there a reason *not* to buy one of these for their kids. It was great for us when you showed them how fun these things could be, but when you rolled it, every parent in there saw their kids doing that same thing. Two thousand moms in Erie now have veto power when their husbands try and buy one of these for their kids."

It made sense, but chuck-a-puck would never be the same after that. As we stood there, considering the wrecked ride, I'm sure we were thinking about very different things. He was probably trying to come up with a story for his boss, one that would explain the wrecked four-wheeler on the shop floor in the morning, hoping it'd be convincing enough to ensure that he still had a job. I, on the other hand, just stood there thinking, "Damn. Now I have to come up with a new gimmick."

***

Chuck-a-puck sucked without my between-period ride. People had been conditioned. They had expectations. Now, when they swung open the doors for the Cycle City plows, I moseyed out onto the ice behind them and waited for the announcer to count it down.

"3—2—1. Let 'em have it!"

Most of the pucks arched high, like arrows loosed from the Elven archers defending Helm's Deep. They rained down as before, only this time I was without any real defense. Instead of one or two glancing blows, like I had experienced before, I took one direct hit after another. In honesty, most were ineffectual. Yes, they hit me in the eyes and teeth—or rather Shooter's eyes and teeth. Mostly they bumped and jarred me less than the actual crowd when I climbed around in the stands. A few hit home, though—one right in the breadbasket—and as any guy might tell you, it doesn't take much for you to feel *that*.

I doubled over when that first puck made contact, exposing then my unprotected lower back. More than one found my healing, but still very tender, sacral contusion, and that sent me to the ice in earnest.

I crawled to the player benches and took what refuge I could against the wall, exposing myself to projectiles from just one side of the arena. The good news was that most of them had terrible aim and lacked the muscle to inflict much harm on me while I was there.

Waiting for the waves of pain to subside from my stomach and lower back, my gloved hand found a large pile of soft snow. It was right at the small door where players stopped themselves on their way into the bench area. As I gripped it, I noticed, unlike the snow outside in the dead of winter, this snow was quite sticky: perfect for making forts and snowmen—and snowballs.

The crowd had exhausted their ammunition by this point, so I hurriedly stockpiled my own ammo. When the plows moved forward to clear the ice, I made my move. Climbing into the bench area, I hurled snowballs at the unsuspecting crowd, raining wet terror upon them as the little cowards ducked and covered. When it was time for the ice to be resurfaced, I took the fight into the stands themselves, carrying a small supply of snowballs with me. I struck a kid in the gut, nailed the back of a bald man's head, and showered a group of unsuspecting college kids.

Snowball fights. It was simple, something we'd all done as kids. And now, after every period, I knew where I could find a ready supply.

The next game, after I discovered the snowballs, I reported to work as usual, when Brent pulled me aside.

"Did you see it?"

"See what?"

"The article?" Brent said simply. "About that billet family came down from Guelph for the game the other day. The ones you hit with a bunch of snowballs."

"Oh—really?"

"Yeah," he said. "They wrote a nasty letter to the editor, talking about how they had never been so disrespected. Apparently, you were rude and vulgar and attacked their whole family maliciously."

"But it was just snow. I'm sure they've thrown their share up in Canada," I said. "And besides, it's not like I could see well enough through that mask to target anyone specifically."

"I know, that's what I said when they called for comment," Brent shook his head. "I said that Shooter throws snowballs at some point in nearly every game and there was certainly nothing malicious about it."

For a moment, I hesitated. That game was the first time that I had thrown any sort of snow into the crowd. Granted, I didn't intend to target fans of the opposing team. I was simply returning the favor to a crowd who saw fit to pummel me with pucks when I no longer had any means of evading them.

"But, Brent, I never—"

"Shooter throws snow," he cut in, "at *every* game."

So, I did, from that point on. At least once in the lull between periods, I constructed a small arsenal of snowballs and threw, almost without impunity. Mostly, I zeroed in on areas of the stands frequented by season ticket holders, though it was indeed difficult to target any one person directly. Then again, in the sea of blue and yellow jerseys, one thing started to stand out—anyone wearing the colors of the opposing team. Yes, I mostly hit my own. But thanks to that letter to the editor, I always saved a few and made a concerted effort to welcome those who made the drive in from out of town.

Trading Up

Brent, the man who gave me my first break as a mascot, left the field of sports management in the fall of 2003. He was replaced by a dynamic duo of women. They split his duties. Angela, a recent graduate from one of the local colleges, took over his day-to-day job as director of marketing, while Erin, a fun intercollegiate import from Alberta, Canada, took over Brent's game day promotions as a marketing intern.

The impact that this change of management offered was apparent immediately. During my first season with the Otters, Brent seemed good enough at his job, but that was mainly my inexperience talking. In hindsight, the marketing and promotions activities that I had been a part of for the first year felt more like a frat party than anything that resembled business. Things that were fun got done, and everything that was expensive or inconvenient was tabled for another day. For example, when Brent was running the show, I had grown accustomed to the sensation of burning nostrils inside a suit so rank that it drew comments from nearly everyone I met. The words "Ugh, Shooter needs a bath" echoed from many a wayward mother, cringing as they watched their kids hugging an odiferous me. This was likely due to the fact that the tattered pelts and head were laundered the first week of every month, regardless of how much it had been used. As you might guess, this was not enough, especially during the lengthy OHL season. The suit wasn't just disgusting. In one very specific instance, it had become a health hazard.

Back in the middle of my first season, I was juggling a full course load at Edinboro University, and because of my course load, I was unable to attend a few promotions that Brent had organized in the afternoons. Luckily, he found a replacement. Someone he knew had a teenage son who happened to be off school one day. Without considering why a kid wasn't attending school on weekday in February, Brent gladly tossed the kid $25 and the suit one afternoon. Only after the fact did I learn that my substitute was home from school due to a persistent case of mononucleosis. When I put on the suit for a game later that evening, it was still inundated with my replacement's sweat from earlier that day. Fast forward a few days and I was crouched in the back stairwell of the Tulio Arena, struggling to breathe and begging for the sweet relief of death.

As you might know, mononucleosis has long been known as "kissing disease." At the time, I felt cheated that I couldn't have contracted this illness in a more traditional way. Of course, I couldn't become infected during a hot date with someone who couldn't keep their hands off me. Nope, I had to contract mono from an unlaundered, sweat-soaked mascot suit.

When the illness, set in, I battled through a few games, struggling to breathe inside that disgusting suit, until one of the ushers found me—gasping for breath, apparently incoherent in the back stairwell. After my visit to our local Urgent Care, the diagnosis was made. When I called the office to explain that I'd have to take a few games off, citing the physician's concern about potentially rupturing my spleen, Brent sighed.

"Yeah, that's probably my fault," Brent said. "I guess Sam had it when he was in the suit earlier this week. Probably should have had Shooter cleaned after that, or something."

Needless to say, Angela had a very different management style than Brent, and to truly see the difference, I had to look no further than Shooter and the plastic dry-cleaning bags that held him at the start of every homestand. Between every series of home games, after every promotion, Angela saw to it that Shooter had a much-needed bath. This was as much to their benefit as my own, but it was still a meticulous detail that felt like a massive improvement.

Despite Brent's departure from the world of sports (opting for a mid-level management job with the local beverage distributor), he still attended the odd hockey game. Often, he came with his new wife, sitting high in the arena at center ice. One night, he was accompanied by a short, redhaired man.

His friend had a round face and a grin that resembled a young Mickey Rooney—if Mickey Rooney had a habit of chewing tobacco. When he saw me in the section below is, he called me up.

"Hey, Shooter," Brent said, reaching out to shake my gloved paw. "Got someone here you might want to meet."

My attention shifted to the man beside him, spitting a brown, viscous fluid into a mostly empty water bottle. The man twisted the lid back onto the bottle and grinned while reaching out to shake my hand.

"Rick McGill," the red-haired man said. "I worked with Brent over at the SeaWolves."

The Erie SeaWolves was the Minor League Baseball team that played in the ballpark next door. My Dad had taken me to a few games when I was a kid, back when they were part of the New York Penn League as an affiliate of the Pittsburgh Pirates. By the time October of 2003 had rolled around, the SeaWolves had joined the Eastern League and had become the Double-A affiliate of the Detroit Tigers.

"Good to meet you, Rick," I said, breaking mascot etiquette for the brief introduction.

"You too," he grinned.

"So, you left us for the SeaWolves?" I prodded Brent.

"Nah, I worked double duty for a few years. You know—MC for the SeaWolves during the off-season."

"Oh, I gotcha," I said. "Didn't realize you'd be able to do that. Thought one team would be more than enough to keep you busy."

"Busy, yes," Brent said. "But I have student loans and the SeaWolves are always good for a few extra bucks in the summer."

"Ugh," I groaned, trying not to think about the loans I had accepted at the start of the new academic year. "I don't even want to think about my student loans."

"Yeah, well, anyway," Brent changed tact. "I was telling Rick about some of the things you do around here. Thought he'd come out and have a look. Alright to give us a show?"

"No problem," I said.

I had enough positive feedback from fans to know what my biggest hits were during any given game. So, as a favor to Brent, I wandered down the steel stairs cattycorner from them, the nearest ones that offered a straight shot to the plexiglass boards. When the puck was iced, I stomped on the steel, calling attention to the section, and when the crowd started clapping along, I did my classic somersault down the stairs. The section erupted in cheers as I slammed into the wall and accepted my accolades before sending a salute in Brent's direction and ducking back into my dressing room for a quick breather.

The rest of the game was fairly normal. A pee-wee hockey league was booked for a short exhibition game between two of the periods, and they skated about on the ice until I began chucking snowballs at them. They retaliated by "pretending" to beat me up with their sticks at center ice before the Zamboni was brought out to prepare the surface for the main event. I tossed souvenirs into the crowd, signed autographs, and took pictures—until the final whistle blew and I retreated into my dressing room for a postgame shower. Once I was sufficiently clean—or as clean as anyone could be showering in that dank, little room—I hit Shooter with some Febreze and hung him up to dry. I returned my key to the front office and headed for my car. I usually parked in the lot behind the arena, where the visiting team's tour busses were often parked.

My wet hair froze quickly in the late-autumn air as I made my way to my car out back. I was halfway across the parking lot when I noticed someone following me. I stepped more quickly then. So did the person following me. I rummaged in my pocket for my car keys and whipped them out. By the time I had my key in the lock of my driver's side door, whoever it was had caught up. A fist fell hard against the trunk of my car and the resulting bang caused me to jump.

I whirled around, thinking that I was about to be mugged, but I was surprised to see that it was just Rick.

"Hey, Shooter," he said, gripping a souvenir hockey stick in his hands. In the dark he looked like a mini mobster explaining to a renegade shopkeeper what could happen if they fell further behind on the protection payments.

"Oh, Rick, right?" I said, unlocking the door.

"Yeah. Hey, just wanted to say—nice work in there tonight. Wish we had someone like you over at the SeaWolves."

"Thanks, I appreciate that."

Although I usually didn't mind chatting with people after a game, this was not one of those nights. It may have been the cold that was now biting at my damp skin and scalp, or perhaps the appearance of a leprechaunish man brandishing a hockey stick like a miniature shillelagh, but whatever it was, I was tired and ready to go home. I dropped into the driver's seat, but before I could pull my door closed, Rick stepped in front of it.

"By the way, what would it take to make that happen?"

"What?"

"Getting you to work with us next season," Rick said. "What would it take?"

I slid the keys into the ignition and the engine turned over. Then, I cranked on the heater. The cold air blew from the vents, and I knew it would take a few minutes for my car to warm up, especially with the cold air rushing in through my open door.

"Brent already told me what they're paying you," Rick said. "Shame, really. For everything that you do. I mean, you're easily worth an extra ten or fifteen bucks a game." He adjusted the grip on his hockey stick and glanced down at me from the corner of his eye. "Would that do it?"

It took a moment for the offer to set in. The Otters' pay was minimal. At the time, I was making $30 per game, and $25 per promotional appearance. On average, during the season, this job banked me an extra $180 per week, which wasn't going to make me rich by any stretch of the imagination, but it was a nice supplemental income. During off nights, I still worked Chuck E. Cheese, but at that wage, I'd bank roughly the same money whether I worked three to four hours at a hockey game or slung pizzas for eight hours. Rick's offer wouldn't change the equation too much, and apparently it showed.

"What are you thinking?" Rick asked.

I was a year into my first job as a sports mascot. I didn't know anyone else in that line of work, so I had no idea what the going rate should be.

"I'm not sure," I answered.

"Come on," Rick said. "Shoot me a number."

I hesitated. "Don't you already have a guy?"

"We had to cut him loose," Rick said. "Actually—in all honesty—he quit, but only because we wouldn't play his little game."

"What game was that?"

Rick shrugged. "Last year, the *Times* did a story on him, a sort of 'C. Wolf behind the scenes' thing. It gave him an inflated ego."

"So, what? He wanted more money?"

"That's part of it. Mostly it gave him the false impression that he was irreplaceable. He tried to use that story as validation that he deserved more money. I told him what our budget would allow and he countered with a number from some other planet. Total nonstarter. Just wasn't going to happen."

"So, he's gone for good?"

"Depends," Rick said. "What are your long-term goals? Are you happy with this as a job, or are you interested in making this a career?"

Once Again, my mind shot back to the essay I had written as a joke for my high school Spanish class, declaring my desire to be a professional mascot. Now the joke was on me. I sat in a freezing car, staring up at a Lilliputian man blocking my door open, and yet I was asking myself questions that I hadn't seriously considered before: Would I want to be a professional mascot? Was I even capable of it?

"I haven't really thought about it," I said.

"Well," Rick said, frowning slightly. "There is only so much you can do inside a hockey arena. And Major League teams don't usually consider applicants for mascot operations without at least some baseball experience."

Major League teams? Now that the thought was there, it was certainly an interesting prospect. There was a mystique about working in professional sports, and that was largely the reason I originally accepted the position with the Otters when Brent offered it to me. Then again, I had no idea what it would take to get myself to the next level.

"Maybe I just want a job while I'm going to school?" I said, more a question than answer. "I mean, I might want to actually use my degree when I'm done."

"And if that's the case, you'll need work in the summer too, right? The way I see it, if you like what you're doing, why not take it on in the summer too? Saves you from working other shit jobs in the off-season. Plus, it looks great on the resume, especially if you're looking to stick around Erie after college. You'd be like a local celebrity, times two. Who in town wouldn't want to hire you after this, especially if you do a good job for us?"

It seemed a fair point. Overall, Rick's proposal appeared to be a win-win. Despite the physical demands of the job, I didn't mind this type of work. It kept me in pretty good shape and the money he was offering wasn't terrible.

"Do you think they'd care?"

"Who?"

"The Otters."

"I'm sure they'll be fine with it," Rick finally answered. "A lot of people working in the minors take on multiple jobs. Even our players—professional athletes—sometimes work shit jobs in the off-season. But it's understood when the league minimum's only about a thousand bucks a month. We got guys with massive sign-on bonuses and guys working for peanuts. In this world, there's no shame in taking on other jobs to make ends meet. And wouldn't you rather be doing something that you enjoy?"

I tried to calculate what I'd need to make in the summer. "How many games are there?"

"Thirty-six home games, give or take. Plus promotions."

The heat finally seeped through the vents in my car. As I watched the windshield defrosting, a few numbers rushed through my mind. "Fifty per game, thirty per hour for a promotional appearance."

Rick grinned and gave me a quick nod. With a wink he pointed at me with the handle of his souvenir stick. "Welcome aboard, Shooter," he said. "Or should I say, C. Wolf?"

Twenty-One

Where were you when you turned twenty-one?

This is a question that most Americans of my generation could readily answer, given our social predilection for alcohol and how legal consumption of it coincides with our twenty-first birthdays. While in college, I attended many of my friends' twenty-first birthdays, and I remember many of them well—given that I was usually one of the youngest in my peer group. I attended the dinners, the parties, and was the designated driver at many a birthday pub crawl. Sipping sarsaparilla and sweet tea at the bar, I watched my friends come of age, all the while looking forward to the day when I would be able to join them.

Working in professional sports was grueling and it often meant I had little control over my own schedule. When the team was in town, I worked, and the league directors rarely consulted the mascots to avoid personal conflicts when scheduling games. Moreover, if a promotional event was scheduled, I usually had to attend, unless I could find someone to fill in at short notice (which was rarely easy). Any time any member of the community called with a gimmick or fundraiser, requesting an appearance by C. Wolf, I generally had to show up. When the team was in season, I had no sick days, no vacation days, and no viable excuses. Such is the life of a local pseudo-celebrity. Sure, you have the spotlight on you, but this does not come without sacrifices.

It was the start of my first season as C. Wolf and you can imagine how disappointed I was to learn that my twenty-first birthday fell on a game day. My friends wanted to go out and celebrate, and they had plans long before they shared any of them with me.

Back in college, the ringleader of my small group of friends would have to have been Michelle. I met her my freshman year. Michelle had long brown hair with natural curls. She had intense blue eyes, a perpetual smile, and more energy than I would have thought humanly possible. Michelle was an effortless straight-A student, easily the smartest person in our eclectic band of personalities. Apparently without a need to study, she had assumed the role of organizer, planning all of our social adventures, including parties. As excited as I was for my own birthday, it is quite possible that Michelle had been looking forward to that day even more.

"First, Applebee's," she told me. "We'll have dinner, then we'll hit Peccadillo's and work our way down to the bay."

"I can't," I sighed. "I've got a game."

"Sorry, Denial," she said, always calling me by my college nickname. "But what kind of friend would Ol' Shellerz be if I didn't throw you a party?"

"We can do something next week, while the team is out of town."

"No. You only get those free drinks day of. Delay and we'll have to pay for you to puke. No sir, Denial. It's your birthday and we're cheap. You're having a party that night. Tell Rick that he can throw some other peon in that stupid suit for one day."

"That's not how it works," I sighed.

"That is how it works. Trust me. Ol' Shellerz knows how to play the free booze game."

"No, not the drinks," I said. "I mean the job. Finding a replacement, it's just not that easy."

"Denial, I've seen what you do," Michelle said. "It ain't that hard. Give the popcorn guy ten bucks, then stuff him in the suit, and nobody needs to know."

For most of my life I took the path of least resistance. I was the rule follower. I never tried any type of drug, never tasted alcohol to that point, and though I had friends who enjoyed the occasional whippet, whipped cream was something I generally reserved for pumpkin pie. The reasoning behind my abstinence up until that point was simple: I was perhaps the least lucky person that I had ever known. If someone was going to get caught playing hooky or doing something irresponsible, unethical, or illegal, it would definitely be me.

"If I call off, I might not have a job to go back to," I said simply. "And I kind of need this job now."

"Denial, I'm tellin' you this as a friend. Your job, it kinda sucks."

"Careful," I said. "How many tickets did you want for the next homestand?"

"Hey, I only acknowledged that it sucks for you. I never said it didn't have its perks for ol' Shellerz."

Although I was resigned to the fact that I'd have to work, Michelle (probably the greatest friend I had in my life up until that point) didn't give up so easily. When I made it clear that I would have to work on my birthday, she took the inquiry one step further. She called my boss to inform him of this very special day, urging him to let me have the night off so that they could get me "good and drunk."

The next day, when I entered the ticket office, Rick was chatting with Becky (the sales manager) and Regan (the concessions manager). Laughter boomed from Rick's open office door as I passed by, and he turned his attention on me, wiping away his tears in an attempt to compose himself.

"Dude, your friend is hilarious," he said.

"Who?" I asked.

"Some girl. Real fast talker. Introduced herself as *Denial's ol' friend Shellerz*."

"Damn it. What did she do?"

"She just called and told me how important Wednesday was and explained how 'they had plans for her buddy, Denial'—I assume that's you." Rick made air quotes with his fingers as he spoke. "Apparently I have to give you Wednesday night off so that they can get you 'good and drunk.' I think those were her exact words." Rick chuckled and shook his head. "That Shellerz is quite a character."

"Yeah," I sighed. "That sounds like her."

For a moment I stood waiting for Rick to continue with the story. He just sat there, shaking his head, wide grin splitting his rather pink face.

"So?" I finally asked him directly. "What'd you say?"

"About what?"

"Wednesday," I began. "Can I have it off?"

He raised his eyebrow and scoffed.

"Hell no," he said simply. "You're C. Wolf, man. You're the face of this organization. Think Curtis Granderson could get a night off just so he could go get drunk with some friends? No. He couldn't. Because the two of you are professionals."

***

When Wednesday came, it began like any other game before. I mingled with the crowds, visited the groups who had rented the suites along the third base line, and signed countless souvenirs along the concourse by the front gates. When the game finally started, I reported to the usual place behind the third base dugout where Rick and the Diamond Girls were reviewing the scheduled promotionals and skits that we'd be performing between innings.

"C. Wolf," Rick said, drawing my attention. "You'll need a set of cheer sticks for the bottom of the third for 'Wipeout.' Caitlin will find the bald guys for you and she'll meet you on the third base dugout. But don't drag your feet. Got something special planned for the top of the fourth, so get a move on when you're done."

I looked at the agenda and saw that the fourth inning was blocked off entirely with the words "C. Wolf to RF."

"What's this?" I asked, holding the sheet out for Rick to see.

"RF?" Rick asked, squinting at my schedule. "It's baseball. RF means right field."

"Yeah," I said. "I know that. But why am I going to right field?"

"You're not," Rick said. "You're meeting *me* behind the right field bleachers."

"Okay, but why?"

"Don't worry about it. Just get your ass over to the right field bleachers by the top of the fourth inning. But also, remember, you'll have to drag ass again at the top of the fifth for your basketball stunt on field. Then there's the stampede in the sixth."

Rick continued to run through the itinerary for the game, assigning duties to each of the Diamond Girls to fetch props and recruit unsuspecting fans for some humiliating hijinks, but his lack of explanation for the fourth inning was uncharacteristic. Usually, Rick's itineraries were extremely detailed, dictating precisely where I had to be and when, along with a description of what I needed to be prepared to do. The lack of detail, combined with the fact that I had never been summoned to do anything in the right field bleachers before, left me reasonably confused. Still, one thing was apparent. This was going to be a busy day for me.

I followed along in the itinerary, popping up on the dugout for my introduction during the bottom of the first inning. Then, I made my rounds to the luxury boxes for photo ops for the corporate clients. Next thing I knew, it was time for "Wipeout."

The skit itself was simple—but it remained one of my favorites. Before it started, the Diamond Girls found two very shiny-headed, bald men in the crowd and offered them a small bribe—two reserved seat tickets to a future game of their choice—for their participation. Once accepted, the young girls led these unsuspecting men down to one of the dugouts, with a pair of folding chairs, where I would be waiting with two inflatable cheer sticks. While game play continued, I stood on the railing between sections, arms flailing, cheer sticks banging, until the final out sent the teams scurrying to and from their respective benches. The Diamond Girls placed the chairs on the dugout and the two men clamored up and sat, glancing nervously at one another, just as a shrill voice giggled "Hee-hee-hee-hee, Wipeout."

As the drum solo sounded over the speakers, I snuck up behind one of the men and pounded on his head with the cheer sticks, in synch with the audio. Cue the guitar riff and I danced around to the opposite side of the dugout taunting the crowd, until the next drum solo approached and I continued my shtick, working both bald heads like a drum set, ending with a flourish that sent the cheer sticks into the crowd before us. A quick handshake and photo with our victims, and Caitlin mouthed what was next for me—RF.

I threaded myself through the crowd that had amassed near the concession stands. I did my best to push through them, pausing here and there to greet any kids I met along the way. Finally, as I neared the right field bleachers, I saw Rick and Regan leaning against the perimeter fence behind the stands. They waved me over, and I slipped behind the crowd and followed them around back. There, tucked beneath the bleachers, was a walk-in refrigerator, one of the few that I had never visited before.

When the temperature inside the suit climbed to some unbearable level, I often shuffled over to the nearest concession stand, ducked into the cooler, removed C. Wolf's head, and settled onto the floor between pallets of hotdogs and chicken wings. In the cold, I'd catch my breath and cool off to the intermittent shush of beer shooting through tapped kegs along the far wall.

But while the other coolers were easily accessible during games, the one beneath the right field bleachers had a handle that was secured by a large padlock. I had never seen anyone go in or out of this cooler during games before, but that was about to change. The lock fell off into Rick's hand and he pulled the handle. The hinges of the door squealed as it swung open.

"Come on in, C. Wolf," Rick said, motioning me up the ramp and inside.

Immediately the reason for the lock was clearly apparent. This refrigerator served just one purpose—it stored the bulk of the beer. Along one wall, there was a row of silver kegs; along the other, stacked on pallets, were several cases of canned and bottled beverages. I removed C. Wolf's head as Regan pushed by me and moved to the very rear of the cooler. He returned a moment later to the doorway, where Rick and I had been standing, with three sixteen-ounce cans. He handed one can to Rick, who opened it, and another to me. I eyed the two of them suspiciously.

"You're kidding right?"

Rick glanced at me, then down to my unopened beer.

"Regs," Rick said. "Look at him for a moment and think."

Regan popped the top of his beer, then considered me. My fuzzy four-fingered paw wrapped around the can.

"Shit, sorry, C. Wolf," he said, wincing slightly. "Let me help you with that."

With his free hand, the concessions manager reached over and cracked open the beer for me. Then, he and Rick smiled and the two of them tapped their cans against my own.

"Happy birthday, C. Wolf," Rick said.

Both he and Regan took a long swig from their cans. Then, a little hesitantly, I tipped the contents of the first beer I would ever drink into my mouth. The moment the liquid touched my tongue, I wanted to spit it out. It tasted like fermented cat pee. It was sour and skunky, leaving me with an aftertaste that had me rethinking the whole notion of alcohol. I felt my face contort as I choked it down. Rick and Regan laughed.

"Well, what do you think?" Rick asked, taking another swig from his own can.

"Not what I expected, to be honest."

"Yeah." Regan wrinkled his nose and nodded apprehensively. Then he lifted the can and glanced at its bottom. "This isn't the best stuff."

It really wasn't. But, given that this was my very first beer and that my boss had just given me an inning of the game off to drink on my birthday, I just smiled, shrugged, and choked down another mouthful, accepting the gesture for what it was. Rick chortled as he took his next sip.

"What's so funny?" I asked.

"Nothing, just remembered something." Rick took another sip from his beer. "Did I ever tell you how C. Wolf got his voice?"

I thought for a moment and then answered, "I don't think so."

If you ever attended an Erie SeaWolves game between 2000-2006, you might have noticed one thing that set C. Wolf apart from other mascots. No, it's not the creepy smile, or his unblinking stare—those are the industry standard. It is not the stupid stunts, the costume changes, or the way that he fires that T-shirt cannon. No. At that time, he was notorious for being the only mascot in the United States—nay, the world—who talked. It was enough to give the mascot union rep an aneurism, but it's true. What was not widely known was the legend of how C. Wolf ultimately found his voice.

"Believe it or not," Rick told me, standing just inside the door of the right field beer cooler, "we haven't always had the best luck recruiting for C. Wolf over the years. You might not realize it, but people aren't exactly falling over themselves, knocking the office door down for the chance to do this job."

"Oh, really?" I fixed him with my best say-it-ain't-so expression. "I'm shocked."

"Well, the point is, the franchise has been here for nine years, and we've had more than twice that many wolves. Over that time, we've had a few go bad."

"Bad how?"

"Nothing too crazy," Rick said. "Usually, they'd just go rogue on us. They'd break some long-established rule—jump on the field during play, steal someone's hat and throw it over the fence—that sort of thing. That's how he learned to talk."

I hesitated. "Yeah?"

"C. Wolf didn't always talk, you see. A few C. Wolfs ago, we had a guy who—well—was a bit of a drinker. He started drinking on the job. You know, stone sober in the first inning, a little clumsy by the third—after the fifth inning he was pretty hammered. Thing is, when he drank, he had this tendency to get rather loud. He'd harass the opposing team's players. One time a player almost came up off the field when C. Wolf said something about his mother while he was on deck. Eventually, he got real flirty with a few girls, and nearly got his ass beat by someone's boyfriend. After that, we couldn't keep him on as C. Wolf, you see."

"That makes sense."

"So, we moved him to concessions and—"

"Wait. You kept him on?"

"Oh, yeah," Regan cut in. "He carries the keg backpack now—generates more in drink sales than anyone else in the stadium."

"Hold up," I said, shaking my head at the irony. "He had a drinking problem, and you actually strapped him to a keg and sent him out to wander the stadium?"

"Well, he's got to account for the beer. Either he gets other people to buy it or he has to pay the difference out of his pocket. It's a motivator."

I squinted at Regan, attempting to detect a hint of deception. It never came.

"Anyway," Rick said, "we found someone else to fill out the suit. But then all the fans complained. Turns out they really loved that loudmouthed wolf. So, to appease them, we started letting C. Wolf talk, and he's been that way ever since."

"That can't be true," I said.

"Oh, but it is," Rick said with a wink, then added, "Far as you know."

When the last out was called over the radio, we chugged the last of our beers and handed the empty cans to Regan to dispose of and I pulled on C. Wolf's head. Perhaps it was psychological, but I felt the effects of the alcohol coming on. I was a little lightheaded and felt unbalanced at first as I stepped back out into the light of the setting sun.

"So, what'd you think?" Rick asked, lacing the padlock back through the refrigerator's handle. He snapped the shackle closed and tugged on it twice for good measure.

"It was a memorable first beer, for sure," I said. "But it kinda tasted the way pee smelled."

"Yeah," Rick said. "Don't let this one put you off the stuff. There is a lot better beer out there."

"What would you guys recommend?"

"Anything else, really," Regan answered, glancing to the bottom of one of the empty cans as he carried them to the nearest recycling bin and tossed them in. As he turned back, I fixed him with a curious stare. Then, remembering that he couldn't see my face, I cocked my head to the side and scratched the top of C. Wolf's head in an inquisitive sort of way.

"Personally," Regan continued. "My only preference is beer that isn't two years past its drink-by date."

I threw my paws in the air and shook C. Wolf's head in disbelief. When I answered, I did so in C. Wolf's gruff, piratey growl. "You mean to tell me that beer was expired?"

"Don't worry," Rick said. "They're safe to drink, just a little skunky is all."

"Why?"

"Well, it's your first beer," Regan cut in, "so we really didn't think you'd notice. Second—I know it's your birthday, and we want you to have a good time and all, but you're an employee and I have my beverage costs to consider."

As I stood there, trying to formulate a suitable response, Rick bopped C. Wolf on the back of the head.

"C. Wolf, that's the second out. Basketball skit—go."

Furry Felonies

In 2004, Rick, beckoned me into his office just before the start of a game. His shelves were lined with limited edition memorabilia—bobbleheads, signed balls, and souvenir bats—all products of his tenure with the organization. On the opposite wall, life-sized posters hung depicting some of the team's most promising prospects from the past several years—Kenny Baugh, Max St. Pierre, and Joel Zumaya.

I occupied a stool, the only seat capable of accommodating my tail. As he closed the door, he lowered himself into the vinyl office chair behind his desk. He scooted close and leaned in. There was a conspiratorial glint in his eye, and his breath smelled of mint tobacco when he spoke.

"I need a straight answer," he began with a tone of mock sincerity. "What are you willing to do for this club? Any limitations, you better tell me now."

The question itself caught me off guard. Afterall, I was just a jester, a hired hand who hammed it up for the crowd on game nights. Questions of loyalty were irrelevant. This was a job—it paid my bills.

"I'm not sure what you mean."

"Well," Rick continued. "Would you be willing to 'apprehend' a few of our competitors—put them out of commission ahead of this next road trip? You know—get the bad juju going for their team?"

"You're suggesting?"

"Kidnapping," Rick said. "More precisely—kidnapping Steamer and Diesel Dawg in Altoona."

Steamer and Diesel Dawg were the mascots for the Altoona Curve, our biggest rival in the league. Steamer, shaped like a giant, green Erlenmeyer flask, was allegedly a boiler from one of the locomotives that trolled the horseshoe curve that ran around the city in Altoona, Pennsylvania. Not exactly the kind of mascot I'd have expected. On the other hand, Diesel Dawg was exactly what I'd expect. He was giant dog who wore an engineer's hat and bandana.

As soon as Rick mentioned Steamer and Diesel Dawg, I understood what he meant. All this was just scripted hijinks. Rick was trying to get a rise out of me. Now that I understood, I decided it was best to play along. But what was the best way to respond when your boss asked you to commit a felony? After a moment, I did what any self-respecting employee might do in such a situation—I demanded an advance.

***

The next time the team left Erie, I found myself outside of the Blair County Ballpark in Altoona, PA, lugging an oversized blue and purple bag through one of the stadium's staff entrances. A woman named Ceana led me through the main concourse to the front offices. Along the way, plastered all over the ticket windows, front gates, and support columns were wanted posters from the Altoona Police Department. According to the brief narrative, a six-foot-tall wolf had accosted two of the most "beloved" mascots in baseball.

Steamer and Diesel Dawg had not been seen around the ballpark since. One local television studio claimed to have the "treacherous crime" on video, and select televisions around the stadium were looping the grainy footage of two oversized, awkward—perhaps drunken—Muppet-like creatures, bumbling around the empty parking lot after dark. From out of nowhere, a white van screamed into view and a fuzzy, gray, four-fingered paw hoisted them inside. The door slammed, and it sped away. The prime suspect of it all: the diabolical, sinister, no-good mascot—C. Wolf.

Little did I know, at a news conference earlier that day, the police found a young boy who could crack the case wide open. Conner was five years old, and there was nothing he'd rather do in the world than fight crime. Recognizing Conner's natural talent, the chief of police deputized him and welcomed him onto the force with an authentic badge. Still, the police chief was at a loss. No resources possessed by the Altoona Police Department would be any match for a giant, six-foot-tall, baseball-playing wolf. But then, as though called into action by hopeless circumstances, the blue and yellow power rangers arrived to provide their expertise. Conner donned the red ranger's jumpsuit and mask, and was charged by the chief of police to lead a special investigation to pursue and capture the diabolical fugitive known only as C. Wolf.

In the front office, Ceana, an intern in her early 20s, briefed me on the current events. She was my mole, the spy strategically placed in Altoona to aid and abet me in my felonious efforts. Ceana was slender with long, tousled blonde hair and she smelled strongly of peppermint—which was distinctively different and much more pleasant than the scent of mint tobacco that hung around Rick back in Erie.

"In something like this," Ceana began with a Cheshire grin that exposed every one of her artificially white teeth, "there are no rules. Your goal is to evade—until the seventh inning. Then, you'll need to be here."

She opened a map of the ballpark and indicated a small area behind the outfield wall.

"That's where we'll stash Steamer and Diesel Dawg. There's a trap door there that you can come through. They usually use it to send a dancer out onto the field when there's a home run. Anyway, you'll go through there, but be careful. The power rangers are going to be right behind you."

"Is there anything in particular you need me to do until then?" I asked.

"Whatever you want," she said. "It's your house. Just be sure you're there by the seventh. I'll take care of the rest."

I accepted my instructions and thanked Ceana for her help. In return, she pulled me in for an unusually tight hug. It was something I was not accustomed to. True, while I was inside the suit, random strangers hugged me all the time, but without the shield of the suit, having someone pull me in for a genuine hug felt strange, almost alien.

Ceana stepped outside and closed the door of the conference room. I slipped into C. Wolf and did my best to prepare myself for what would be one of the most interesting experiences of my short career.

When I emerged next, Ceana was waiting for me just outside the door. She led me through a room of cubicles down some hallways. Outside the elevator, I caught Ceana eying me. I wasn't quite sure what to make of it. Was there something wrong with my costume? Was the Velcro strap that held my tail showing? I was just about to ask when she finally broke the silence.

"You know," Ceana said, "I don't often get the chance to meet other wolves around here."

"*Other* wolves?" I asked.

The presence of that single word stood out to me and I wasn't quite sure what it meant.

"Oh," she said. "I didn't tell you. I'm a wolf too."

What did she mean by that? During our conversation when I first arrived, she had shared a few details about herself—mainly that she had lived in Erie as a teenager and she went to school at Penn State Behrend. From that, I reasoned that she must have just been a SeaWolves fan.

I was wrong about that. Just how wrong though? You'll find that out somewhere around Chapter Twelve

On the way out of the elevator, Ceana gave me one more hug, punctuated by a good luck pat on the tail. Although this wasn't the first time that this had happened, there was something different about the way Ceana did it. It seemed almost part pat, part stroke. I wasn't quite sure what to make of it. But soon enough, the pat on the butt and the whole "I'm a wolf too" thing slipped out of my mind, and I prepared myself to face what was bound to be the most hostile crowd of my career.

Actually, I was wrong about that part too. When I first emerged onto the concourse, the jeers that I had expected did not materialize. In fact, children were lining up waiting their turn for a high-five, a hug, or a picture. The fans greeted me with warm, welcoming smiles, posing for photos, and requesting autographs. One little girl, three years old with curls and wearing a T-shirt with Steamer on it, even beckoned me to bend down, and she kissed the eye patch over C. Wolf's left eye—the one that was reportedly knocked out by a rogue foul ball hit by Jose Guillen at the home opener back in 1995. As legend would have it, this was before the team decided to install the backstop behind home plate at Jerry Uht Park.

"Boo boo all better?" she asked in a voice that could melt any heart.

I nodded.

Before the game, I ran about the stadium—occupying random seats, offering a handspring or two in the infield, and harassing anyone who crossed my path in an Altoona Curve baseball cap or jersey. After all, with Steamer and Diesel Dawg incapacitated, this was *my* house, regardless of what any of the wanted posters might imply. Even my team was wearing their home whites, while the Curve sported dingy gray uniforms. Oddly enough, the sentiment that this was my house seemed to be echoed by the fans themselves. The more I taunted, jeered, and harassed them, the more they cheered me on.

Finally, when the game was about to begin, I sought refuge in the bouncy houses along the first base line as Conner and the two power rangers climbed onto the third base dugout. The announcer took to the PA system and informed the crowd of the "dastardly crime" that I had committed. C. Wolf was guilty, or so he seemed to imply, of kidnapping Steamer and Diesel Dawg.

So much for a fair trial, I thought.

Conner and the other rangers began their pursuit in earnest then. I remembered Ceana's instruction to evade until the seventh inning, so I did just that. I bounced with a few kids in the bouncy house with a giant likeness of Steamer on top of it. That is until I saw the blue and yellow rangers enter the kid zone. Immediately I hopped out, waggled my fingers at the tip of my long, wolfy snout, and sprinted toward the fence just as a final out was made and the outfielders began trotting into their dugout. I leapt the fence and ran to the SeaWolves' dugout where the "power punks" could not follow. It was as if I was Goldar, and the dugout was Rita Repulsa's moon base. Once there, the rangers would not—or perhaps could not—pursue.

I hunkered down there for a bit, until I noticed one of the players exiting the stadium through a door in the back wall. At my home stadium, there were no doors in dugouts. The clubhouse was located in the Erie Civic Center, and getting there involved a long walk across the outfield. But here, a door in the back of the dugout led to a network of concrete hallways. It was getting hot, and I needed a break, so I followed this player through the door, removed my head, and ambled through the underbelly of the stadium.

The ballgame progressed quickly, and before I knew it, I was summoned behind the outfield wall. By the time I arrived, my coconspirator, Ceana, was already wrapping a clothesline around Steamer and Diesel Dawg and positioning them next to a large gray box that contained the power controls for what I think was the scoreboard. With a boost from Ceana, I scurried up on top and struck a menacing pose.

When Conner came into view, he made a beeline straight for my prisoners, never noticing me, perched ominously above them. As he unwrapped the rope from around their chests, the other Rangers finally noticed me.

"Look out!" one of them shouted.

Conner assumed a karate-like pose just as cheers erupted inside the stadium. That should've been the final out in the seventh inning. I looked down at Ceana, who was poised at a small hatch in the outfield wall. That was my cue to take the battle onto the field so that the fans could witness our final, climactic confrontation. I jumped down on the far side of the transformer and waited for Conner to catch up to me. He grabbed me by the arm and flung me through the hatch and I tumbled into the outfield. Behind first base, a convoy of police cars roared through a gate and onto the warning track—lights flashing, sirens wailing. It looked like every patrol car in the city had come out, just for this occasion.

From out of nowhere, Conner emerged with a giant dog catcher's net and he flung it over my head, knocking me to the ground. As I fell, I felt my foot connect with something, and when I looked down, to my horror, it was Conner.

I had just kicked the Make-A-Wish kid.

For a long moment my heart plummeted and I wondered if I had taken this "battle" of ours too far. But when Conner finally rolled back to his feet, he struck another pose for the audience. He might have been ill, but even the sickest of kids are capable of astounding resilience. Two police officers lifted me up and tossed me into the back of an SUV. The door slammed and a heavy hand pounded twice on the rear hatch. There was no escape for me now.

I removed my head and stared out of the tinted glass as this convoy began moving once more. Conner was in one of the patrol units, waving at the crowd, and Steamer and Diesel Dawg bobbled on the back of a golf cart, finally free after a weekend of alleged "torment."

The convoy rolled out of the stadium and onto a narrow service road that connected with the parking lot. One of the police officers opened the rear hatch and I replaced my head for the last time that day.

When I rolled out, Conner was waiting and I knelt beside him. He stared at me with a serious look on his face.

"I love you, C. Wolf," he said. "But you're a bad doggy."

The police officer grabbed one of my arms and locked a pair of handcuffs around my wrist. With my free arm, I covered C. Wolf's eye and cowered in the most pitiful position I could manage. Conner motioned toward Steamer and Diesel Dawg, still poised, motionless, smiling unblinkingly on their golf cart.

"I'm sorry," I said in C. Wolf's pirate-like growl.

Conner looked up at the policeman and said, "It's okay, he's sorry. You can let him go."

"Are you sure?" the officer said. "We can run him downtown."

"No, he learned his lesson."

And with that, the police officer removed my cuffs and I knelt down to offer Conner a long hug of appreciation for his service.

This was Conner's wish. He suffered from a seizure disorder—though I can't recall specifically what it was—and the Make-A-Wish Foundation offered him the chance to live out his dream of fighting crime with the power rangers. As I left the ballpark that day, Conner, Steamer, Diesel Dawg, and a few of the police officers were riding up the white hill of the wooden roller coaster that overlooked the outfield of Blair County Ballpark. I watched them teeter over the crest and rattle their way along the rickety track. And that was the last I ever saw of him. Though I think of him often, I never learned what happened to Conner. I could never bring myself to check.

I like to picture him as a teenager now, sitting atop the Appalachian foothills in the coal country of central Pennsylvania, wondering occasionally who I was—the man who played a wolf one afternoon so he could live his childhood dream. Perhaps he'll read this account of that day and think to himself, *Hey, I think that's me*, and maybe, just maybe, he'll remember how a city of strangers came together to transform him into the hero he was always meant to be.

PNC Park

Baseball—it's the American pastime. At least, it used to be.

There are stories about American naval vessels getting sunk in World War II and as the rescue ships pulled up to fish survivors from the surf, they identified friend from foe by asking one simple question: Who won the World Series? If the survivors answered correctly, they'd run out the lines, drop in some inflatables, and haul them up to safety. One can only wonder what fate would befall those who didn't know the answer. Back then, baseball was such an integral part of American culture, it could literally mean the difference between life and death.

By the time I was a kid, though, the game was falling out of favor. Beyond gym classes and pickup games, I didn't play much growing up, but it didn't stop the daydreaming. Granted, my friends and I loved baseball movies; *Major League*, *Little Big League*, *The Sandlot*, *The Natural*, and *Rookie of the Year* were a few of our favorites. Often, while I watched these movies, I'd slink down to our unfinished basement and pretend that I was Rick "Wild Thing" Vaughn stepping in to warm up my arm before striking out Clu Haywood or Jack Parkman. I blared the theme song from the old eight-track my dad had fixed up and wired under his workbench. I can't tell you how many times I pitched that rubber ball against the cinderblock walls to the beat of that song.

Because I had focused my energy on soccer in my youth, I knew that walking across the infield of a Major League ballpark to the sound of my own theme song was just a fantasy. It could never happen.

***

On June 26, 2004, the Pittsburgh Pirates announced that they would be hosting a "Futures Game" at PNC Park in Pittsburgh. The game itself was intended to give Minor League talent a glimpse of what it would be like to play in a Major League ballpark. On the one hand, it would give the people of Pittsburgh a chance to glimpse the talent that was working its way through the team's farm system. On the other hand, the game offered a lower-stakes orientation of the ballpark to Minor Leaguers, an important opportunity to work through some of the jitters before they found themselves back in Pittsburgh, playing for much higher stakes in the future.

When I returned home from the Make-A-Wish event in Altoona, I was informed that this Futures Game wasn't just an opportunity for the players to flirt with their Major League dreams. It was also an opportunity for the mascots as well. And because that year the game would feature the Altoona Curve and the Erie SeaWolves, it would be an opportunity for me to live out that fantasy I had formed years ago as a kid, pitching my rubber ball against the basement wall.

Rick was the one who shared the invitation with me, in much the same sort of style that he used to inform me of my trip to Altoona.

"It's official," Rick grinned. "Next Saturday, you're heading to The Show!"

"The Show?" I asked.

I had heard this reference before, in movies like *Bull Durham*. Kevin Costner is sitting on the bus with his teammates, trying to explain to a rookie pitcher what it was like to face Major League sluggers. That pitcher sarcastically spits back "You've been in The Show?" to which Kevin Coster's character mutters more to himself than to anyone else, "Yeah. I've been to The Show."

Rick leaned in over his desk and repeated those words. "The Show."

I blinked and shook my head, as though I were trying to dislodge something from my ear. "I'm going to Detroit?"

"No—no. Not Detroit," Rick said. "You're going to Pittsburgh."

Now I was really confused. The SeaWolves were once the Single-A affiliate of the Pirates, but that was when the franchise was first moved to Erie. When it was incorporated into the Double-A Eastern League, the organization affiliated itself first with the Anaheim Angels for a season or two until the Detroit Tigers came along. Since then, the SeaWolves had practically nothing to do with the Pirates organization. Then again, Minor League mascots are not actually a part of the farm system in that same way. Nothing that Rick was saying made sense to me.

"Hold on," I said, flashing Rick the universal signal for timeout. "What are you trying to tell me?"

"You—are—going—to—Pittsburgh—Saturday."

"I'm going to Pittsburgh Saturday?" I asked.

Rick nodded.

"Why?"

"You are going to PNC Park to work as a mascot at a baseball game," Rick said. "Jesus, do I have to spell everything out for you?"

"You're not yanking my chain, are you?"

"No. It's totally legit."

"I'm going to be a mascot at a Pirates game next Saturday?"

"Oh—God no," Rick said, closing his eyes and shaking his head in disgust at the thought. "No. Listen carefully and try not to jump the fucking shark. You—C. Wolf—will be going to PNC Park to work as a mascot during a baseball game." He paused, then added, "A Minor League game—between the SeaWolves and the Curve."

"So—not The Show?"

"It's PNC Park, C. Wolf," Rick said. "It is a Major League stadium. In my opinion, that's The Show. It fuckin' qualifies."

Rick offered me a dumbfounded look that betrayed a hint of a smile and he shook his head. If he had been trying to get a rise out of me, he definitely succeeded. No—I wasn't literally going to The Show just then—but still, I would be working a Major League ballpark—and that at least was something.

"Oh, one caveat," Rick said. "You're going to have to take the bus."

"Wait? The team bus? With the players?"

"No, dammit," he scoffed. "The boosters are going to have a bus. GM says you have to hitch a ride with them. No need for a hotel or gas money for you on this one."

***

The bus pulled into a parking lot near PNC Park a few hours before game time. On arrival, I was ushered inside and led through the bowels of the building, before entering what looked like a small banquet room. Plastic chairs were stacked along the walls, along with a small cluster of folding tables. At one end of the room, a few television monitors glowed with a live image from inside the park where the grounds crew could be seen prepping the infield.

There were two other people already there—a forty-year-old man with graying brown hair and a younger protégé, both wearing Altoona Curve T-shirts. Sitting on the floor next to them were my nemeses—the green shell of Steamer and the deflated pelt of Diesel Dawg.

"Hey, Wolf," the older man greeted, as he continued digging into a plate of vegetables. "Help yourself, why don't you."

He gestured to the far wall to one table that had a generous spread of fruit and vegetable trays and a large bowl filled with bottles of water, heaped over with ice.

"Thanks," I said.

I let C. Wolf and my bag of props fall to the floor, and I crossed the room to claim a bottle of water and to fix myself a small plate to snack on. Then, I settled along the same wall where the other two mascots were sitting. As I munched, the guy who played Steamer handed me a piece of paper.

"Just a heads-up," he said, "We're not going to cross paths out there much today."

"Oh?" I said, sinking my teeth into a piece of fresh pineapple, slurping to keep the juice from dribbling down my chin.

"Yeah, something about the Pirates needing to maintain a 'family-friendly atmosphere'—we've got to keep things G-rated. No fighting, no scrapping. In fact…" Steamer nodded at the paper. "…between-inning activities have all been divvied up. Top goes to us." He paused, chuckling preemptively at the joke he was about to make. "That makes you the bottom. But, hey, we always knew you preferred it that way."

Steamer gave a sideways glance to the kid who would play Diesel Dawg, who, understanding the implication, put his hand over his mouth and giggle-groaned the words "Ah, snap."

I followed, but really didn't care. I was hungry. Because I had ridden down with the boosters, I was forced to skip out on lunch, and this spread they offered here was just what I needed to get through this game. Whether from the Curve or the Pirates, someone was feeding me, and I thought it best not to rock the boat too much. Munching away, I turned my attention to the itinerary Steamer had handed me. The top of several innings had indeed been reserved for "S&D" along with a brief note of what they had planned: "S&D Introductions," "S&D Race," and "S&D Dance Off" stood out to me at the time. The innings that were reserved for me had significantly less detail, reading simply "C.Wolf – TBD."

Usually, Rick and I would chat ahead of the homestands to figure out the skits that we would run during any given game. But as this was not a home game, we had been left largely to the mercy of the staff of the Pirates and the Curve. They were generous enough going into the day—more than generous judging by the food and drinks that they had provided. The organizers had reserved plenty of time for me during the game and appeared to leave a lot of room open for me to figure out what I wanted to do. Luckily, I had come prepared. There were three or four good skits in the extra duffle that I had brought along. It didn't offer quite the flexibility I enjoyed back home, but it would do.

There was a knock on the far door. It opened to reveal the face of a middle-aged man wearing a Pirates polo that seemed to indicate that he worked with the front office staff in some capacity.

"Hey, guys," he said. "Just wanted to know if you wanted a quick tour before game time?"

"Sounds great!" I said, rising and making my way back across the room, though Steamer and Diesel Dawg stayed put.

"We had one earlier," Steamer said. "But you should go."

The man nodded and I followed him into the concrete corridor. As we wandered, he provided a few interesting facts about the stadium. Before I knew it, I was stepping onto the right field warning track, passing just beneath the foul pole.

"This is your most direct point of access. Nobody but staff can get down to the room you're in, so your gear should be safe there while you're out and about."

He walked me down to the dugouts. A few fans were filtering into the seats behind them. My guide led me down into one of them and gestured toward a tunnel that extended through the rear of the dugout.

"This will be the SeaWolves dugout," he said. "This tunnel leads past the locker rooms and connects with that same corridor where your room is located. If you need to, you should be able to gain access to the dugout and field from here."

He led me back through the tunnel and to the holding room where Steamer and Diesel Dawg were now gearing up. I turned my attention back to my unfinished plate, and Steamer gave a little scoff.

"Stuffing your face again, Wolf?"

"No more than you already have, I'm sure," I answered.

"Well don't just sit on your ass down here," he said. "The gates are open and everyone's coming in. We didn't invite you down here so you could lounge around all day. You've got a whole day's work to do before you get paid, you know."

I really didn't have much interaction with Steamer and Diesel Dawg in Altoona, beyond the brief time when our paths crossed when they were bound and gagged behind the outfield wall. But now, the more I talked with the guy behind Steamer, the more irritating he became.

"I'll be out there soon," I said.

"Should've been out there already," he said. "You've got a thing or two to learn if you want to make it in this game, Rook."

"Really?" I said, a little sarcastically.

"Hey, I've got close to ten years in. If you want to be in this game as long as I have been, you might want to watch and take some notes."

Steamer and Diesel Dawg left then, but Steamer's words hung in the air like the smell of the midseason duffle bags of three minor league mascots in an enclosed space. The ego, the jeering…that guy just irked me. I continued eating my way through the plate and drank half of my bottle of water when I saw them bumble across the television monitor. They climbed onto the dugout and walked back and forth a few times, waving occasionally at the people seated in front of them.

I'm not sure what I expected, but it was something more than this. With the guy in Steamer boasting about his "veteran status," I thought he would have done something more, but—no. It was at this point, as I watched Steamer and Diesel Dawg on the monitors, that I resolved that just because I wasn't allowed to openly interact with them didn't mean I couldn't upstage them every chance I got. Luckily, I had some plans. Oh, I'd do what Steamer suggested. I'd watch them every time they went out there. Then I'd raise the bar, one notch at a time.

The first opportunity to upstage the opposition came when I saw their introductions. The stadium was mostly empty, with fans from the two teams concentrated in the seats directly behind each of their respective dugouts. As a result, the PA system seemed to echo more than usual as the announcer named the mascots, Steamer and Diesel Dawg. In response, a camera panned over to Altoona's dugout, and the bulbous boiler and mangy mutt were crawling up on top. Diesel Dawg threw his arms up in celebration and flashed jazz hands to the crowd, receiving a spattering of applause. Steamer bobbed about, throwing his hands behind his back and thrusting his large, hooped belly out to the crowd then he raised his hands triumphantly and nodded to the Altoona faithful, scanning the stands slowly from side to side.

I could do better. Pulling on my head, I grabbed a hula hoop from the collection of props that I brought and marched out of the holding room, making my way to the field.

Between pitches, I crossed the warning track and hopped into the stands, making my way to the friendly crowd behind the first base dugout. As if it were premeditated, a large group of fans howled their greeting. Like any good pack leader, I howled back.

There was a crack of the bat, and a groundball to the shortstop was scooped up and tossed to first base for the third out. We were headed into the bottom of the first.

"He howls, he growls, he bites, and he claws. He's fierce and he's furry, but there's no need to worry. Brought to you by Smith's hotdogs and Pepsi. Give a howl for Erie's favorite mascot," the announcer growled. "C. WOLF!"

Suddenly a familiar baseline, and word echoed across the field in Bono's voice followed by a howl.

"El-e-va-tion! Woo!"

That was my entrance music! Wasting no time, I popped up with my hula hoop and ran down to the dugout and did a traditional handstand entrance, and my fans were loud. Just as the song moved into the first verse, I rolled into a standing position and, off balance, I nearly toppled over into the dugout. Until then, I hadn't noticed just how much more narrow the rooves were in this park compared to my home stadium. Catching myself, I made a mental note of that fact and then proceeded to jump through the hula hoop on the beat of the song until I heard the words "You elevate my soul."
At that cue, I swung the hula hoop down and gyrated my hips, arms in the air clapping on the beat. The crowd before me responded, clapping along with me as I kept the hoop up. Using my tail to my advantage here, I guided the hoop higher on my waist as necessary to keep my hula dance going.

When the music faded and the announcer indicated that the batter was ready for his first pitch, I climbed down from the dugout to the smiles of the SeaWolves Booster Club.

Back in the holding room I dropped C. Wolf's head and chugged another bottle of water, watching the monitors as Steamer thrust his belly forward to the beat of a song. Diesel Dawg responded by sliding on his knees across the dugout, his ears flopping. Steamer countered with a little grapevine and I couldn't help but think how easily I show them up in the next round. Perhaps this competition was all in my head—but even if that was the case—I intended to win it.

Before they had even finished, I was in the stands searching the crowd for someone and my eye landed immediately upon one of the administrative assistants who worked in the front office. She had three kids—including one precocious toddler just under the age of three. After some whispered conversation I had determined that it was time to show off the "Lil' Wolves."

I relayed the message through the powers that be, and the press box prepped the necessary music. Luckily Rick had called ahead so they could queue it up beforehand. Soon, adorable as hell, the Lil' Wolves and I were hunkered down at the end of the first base dugout, waiting for the final out to come. C. Wolf in miniature, each of the one-piece suits had furry gray sleeves and a hood capped with wolf-like ears and pirate hat. Each of the little ones had tails, like mine, but theirs were stitched into the suit, instead of being attached to a belt that ran underneath, and they were much more secure for the effort. The overall effect was not far off from something you'd see in Disney's animated rendition of *Peter Pan*, with the children wearing animal-like pajamas with only their human faces and hands exposed.

"Strike three!" the umpire yelled.

Duran Duran sounded over the PA system, and the familiar drumbeat and guitar riff of the song "Hungry Like a Wolf" echoed across the infield. On cue, I popped up the stairs, the Lil' Wolves on my heels.

We did the usual bit, dance moves that closely resembled those of the "Safety Dance," and the Lil' Wolves chased me in a giant circle when the song rang out with the chorus of "do do dos." Our minutes winding down fast, I

88

decided to try something a little different and finished the bit with three handsprings before ducking back into the dugout. Instead of handsprings, the kids did various clumsy somersaults, and the crowd—even those on the Altoona side—awed audibly.

The game wound down quickly after that. After the seventh inning stretch, Steamer and Diesel Dawg returned to the holding room. I braved the opposing crowd and was greeted well, just as I had been when I visited Altoona earlier in the season. The Curve fans were more than cordial—they were downright warm and jovial. In fifteen minutes of mingling, I signed more autographs and posed for more pictures than at the busiest game I'd ever had in Erie.

By the time I was back in the holding room, Steamer and Diesel Dawg were long gone. The floor looked unusually empty, and the remains of the fruit and vegetable spread had left with them.

After the game, I was so exhausted that it took a while for me to stow C. Wolf and the props in the cargo hold of the booter club's tour bus. Then I climbed the stairs. There was an eerie silence for the first few steps, but as I turned up the aisle the entire bus erupted in a cheer of welcome that was simply staggering. Progressing slowly up the aisle, I shook the hands of every booster who reached out to me, accepting their congratulations and thanks for a "memorable evening." Near the back of the bus, I finally collapsed into an empty seat as the cheers gave way to whispered conversation. At that moment, I was struck by the truth of what Rick had said when he told me I'd be heading to Pittsburgh.

"You're going to The Show," he'd said.

At the time, I didn't think that this would actually qualify, but as the bus pulled away from the stadium, the realization hit me. I had walked the infield of PNC Park, my own theme song filling the space. I was no longer that little boy, pitching balls against a basement wall, dreaming of something that would never happen. No. For that night, I felt every bit the Major Leaguer.

Knockout

Not long after my day at PNC Park, I pulled into the parking lot behind the outfield wall before a game and was surprised to see it filled to capacity with large box trucks, semitrailers, and buses. Normally there was a place for C. Wolf, and the attendant would wave me through without a problem. But not that day.

"Sorry, C. Wolf," the parking attendant said, throwing a thumb over his shoulder. "All full up today."

"Seriously, Dave? Can't spare one spot?"

"Not this time," he nodded in the direction of roadies unloading one of the trucks. "WWE is in town for a house show. They get priority."

"All right, then," I sighed. "See you tomorrow."

With only an hour to spare before the gates were scheduled to open, I was forced into a pay lot at the end of the block. Often those attendants gouged on special event days, and the daily rate ate up half of what I earned as C. Wolf for that game.

I tried to not let it affect my mood as I walked to the ticket office and started toward the dressing room to wake up a freshly laundered C. Wolf. It was there that Rick caught me.

"Hey man, did you hear? WWE is in town," his smiling eyes glinted like a star struck child as he broke the news.

Yeah. And the jerks cost me $20, I thought to myself.

"I heard," I said. "So?"

"So? So, I'm going to run next door and see if I can get someone to throw out the first pitch."

"Like who?"

"Who cares? My only criteria—someone who is on television regularly and on Vince McMahon's payroll. Championship belt optional."

"Okay, but *how* are you going to accomplish this? I mean, you can't just walk into the WWE locker room and grab someone."

"Dude, I'm a marketing director with a professional baseball team," he said, as if title alone gave him an all-access pass to any event in town. "Watch me."

Rick turned and steamed purposefully toward the door.

"All right, man. But you know nobody cares about baseball anymore."

He did not venture a look back, only raised a middle finger in my direction as he rounded the corner and proceeded out the door, vanishing into the crowd that was gathering between the front gates of the ballpark and the entrance marquee of the Tulio Arena.

Just after the gates swung open, I stepped out onto the concourse. Soon an out-of-breath Rick shuffled by, gesturing for me to follow him toward the back door of the ticket office. I wrapped up a few hugs and assured the kids that they'd see me again soon, and followed Rick through the open door and removed my head.

"I got one," Rick said in a haughty tone.

"You got one? Really?" I asked.

"What, you doubted me?"

"All right then, two questions. Who and how?"

"Oh, you'll find out. Just be down in the dugout before the pitch. It's great for publicity. Don't want to miss this."

"Sounds fair. Need anything scripted?"

"Nah," Rick grinned. "I just said we'd wing it. Just make sure you're there for a photo after the pitch."

Obviously, I was curious to see who Rick had recruited for this unique, cross-promotional opportunity. Although I hadn't watched wrestling since the era of Hulkamania, when my older cousin Steven had a penchant for wearing (and ripping off) yellow tank tops before folding me like a pretzel until I could no longer breathe and pinning me against the playroom floor of my grandparents' old farmhouse. Still, I knew what the WWE was and recognized a few of their more prominent stars when I saw them on television, so I was honestly impressed by Rick's ability to convince one of their superstars to grace us with an appearance.

I sat in the dugout waiting for Rick to return with some further direction that never came. Just as the ground crew finished raking the pitcher's mound and spraying water on the infield dirt, the outfield wall opened up, allowing C. Wolf 2 (a white Chrysler minivan with team branding plastered on the sliding door) to roll out onto the warning track. Just then, a shrill sound reverberated across the PA system and the song "All the Things She Said" wailed throughout the stadium. Though I didn't know it at the time, this was the well-known entrance music for a WWE Diva, who happened to be the former WWE Women's Champion. The moment the music hit, the crowd ignited in a way that I hadn't heard before. The yellow lights on the top of the van flashed, as a woman with long dark hair, wearing an oversized SeaWolves T-Shirt popped through the moonroof.

"Ladies and gentlemen," the announcer's voice echoed over the music. "Please welcome tonight's guest who will be throwing out the ceremonial first pitch. Brought to us courtesy of the World Wrestling Entertainment—two time WWE Women's Champion, VICTORIA!"

I perked up in the dugout and watched the van roll along the outfield wall, past the third base bleachers. It came to a stop beside the stowed tarp that rested there at the end of the thirdbase dugout. The entrance music continued as Victoria emerged from the sliding door of the van, leaping up onto the tarp in what appeared to be only that T-shirt and a glittering pair of purple thigh-high boots and matching knee pads.

I stepped up onto the dugout stairs and watched as she solicited screams, whistles, and catcalls from the crowd before hopping off and striding purposefully out to the pitcher's mound. There was a swagger about her. By the way she moved, she seemed to say, *yes, I'm a woman and I'll also knock you the fuck out.*

Victoria took the mound with authority, gripping the ball with a professional three fingered grip. The catcher squatted behind home plate as the music faded away and the crowd simmered slightly. She wound and delivered a ball well within any reasonable strike zone. I took my cue from the subsequent applause and cheers then. I climbed the dugout stairs and walked across the grass to meet Victoria.

She threw both of her hands over her head in triumph while scanning the audience. She seemed not to notice me until she turned and made her way back toward the van. She dropped her chin then and fixed me with a predatory side-eyed glare. We met half-way between the van and pitcher's mound. Her lips tensed and she didn't seem to blink.

I attempted to congratulate her on the first pitch. Usually, the person throwing out the first pitch was eager for a photo or a high five from me. Victoria just stared.

"Yeah! Woo! Nice going!" I shouted, clapped, then raised a paw for a high-five.

Victoria turned, folded her arms across her chest, and considered me for a moment. She rolled her neck, as if she were stretching it before a match. Then, her eyes flickered in the direction of Rick, who was sitting behind the wheel. I followed her gaze and saw him holding his fist out the window. In a smooth deliberate motion, his wrist rotated, shooting her an unmistakable thumbs-down.

Before I could even glance back, it happened. Victoria unleashed an elbow across C. Wolf's plush, pillowy face. Her forearm penetrated the head, tearing the screen that lined the mascot's mouth and jarring my chin. Upon contact, white lights popped throughout my field of vision, and I crumpled to the ground. I felt someone tugging at my leg and rolling me flat on to my back. Then came the pressure of someone's weight on top of me. My knee was drawn to my chest, constricting my breath precisely the way it had been whenever my cousin pinned me in the playroom of my grandparent's farmhouse. In that moment I heard a disembodied voice—a man's voice. It took me a second to realize that this voice was counting.

"One—Two—Three. You got 'em!"

The same entrance music boomed over the PA system, and my vision cleared just in time for me to see a man in a striped shirt raising Victoria's arm in apparent victory. Afterward, she leapt on top of the infield tarp. This time she stripped off the white SeaWolves T-shirt, revealing her coordinated ring gear. She threw the shirt into the stands. For a moment she posed and shouted at the crowd, as if she had just reclaimed her WWE title.

My pulse pounded in my ears and my head throbbed while I watched Victoria taunting the crowd. In the stands, the camera flashes twinkled like distant stars among the sea of people. Then, as quickly as she had come, Victoria ducked back into the van with the referee, which ushered them away. I saw the van proceed through the outfield wall, and Victoria was gone.

Slowly I sat up and hobbled through the gate behind home plate, up the stairs, and to the rear entrance of the ticket office. I removed the lightly damaged head and lay down in the hallway. After some time, the door opened again and Rick ambled over to me.

"DUDE—that was AWESOME!" Rick exclaimed. "I wasn't sure you were going to be able to sell that. But it sure looked like she wrecked you. Damn, how'd you make it look so real?"

I squinted up at him, shielding my eyes from the buzzing fluorescent lights that seemed to be cauterizing a portion of my brain. I started to shake my head but stopped as that only seemed to make things worse. So, I did the only thing I could think of to illustrate my point. I raised the fuzzy middle finger of one of my gray, four-fingered paws.

Apparently, this was hilarious, to Rick. He laughed as I gathered my thoughts and finally asked, "You planned that, didn't you?"

"Of course," Rick said. "You can't just wing something like that when you're working with a professional, like a WWE superstar."

"Could have told me."

"Yeah, but that would have ruined the surprise."

I lay there for a moment, eyes closed, waiting for the headache to fade. "So, how'd you talk her into doing it?"

"Oh, easy. I just went in through the clubhouse. Saw her in that back hallway. There was a dude with a headset back there and I asked him if he'd ask her. And she said yes."

"That's it?"

"Yeah—that's about it. She grew up with some brothers who were into baseball growing up so the whole thing was perfect. And boy did she deliver!"

For a moment, Rick went silent and his mind seemed to wander. I'm not certain exactly what he was thinking about. It could have been her aggression on the mound, the perfect pitch, the elbow in my face, or the posturing on the infield tarp along the third base line.

He let out a satisfied sigh. "She looked great out there, don't you think?"

My head gave another involuntary pulse of pain as I thought about the way her elbow felt against my face and the feeling of her squeezing the air out of my lungs when she pinned me in the infield. I winced.

"Yeah," I finally managed to say. "She's a real knockout."

The Church Picnic

There is never a bathroom large enough—not in this line of work. But of all the restrooms I had ever been confined in, this one was perhaps the worst—a pit toilet with a single graffitied stall and a ceiling that buzzed with yellow jackets in their papier-mâché ball. Fat mosquitos, waiting to feast, clung on to the cracked mirror that had been tagged and re-tagged by rival gangs above a dingy, inoperable sink.

When all was zipped, tucked, and Velcroed, I strapped on the giant wolf head, tucked the empty bag under my arm, and unbolted the door. I stumbled past a crew of disillusioned teens dragging on cigarettes in the narrow shade of the stink house. They had seen me go in with the duffle, and as I passed by them once more in character, they whispered and sniggered in my direction.

It never took parents long to spot me, and this occasion was no different. As soon as I had rounded the corner, a young mother yelled and grabbed her three-year-old daughter by the hand and started dragging her in my direction. I hated when parents did that. The sudden shock of parents grabbing them by the arm was compounded by the presence of an oversized carnivore stalking in their general direction.

"Come on and see the doggy," the mother boomed so assertively that I could hear her clearly from fifty yards away, on the other end of the park.

The child screamed and flailed her arms in a vain attempt to pull away from her mother. Adamant when she drew near enough, the young mother shoved her daughter into me and dug in her pocket for her phone. Just as she was poised to snap a picture, her child rebounded, clawing at her leg in terror.

"What's your problem, girl? You get over there with that doggy so I can get a picture or I'm-a beat yo ass."

The little girl continued to scream, but her mother ultimately got her picture. They almost always did.

This appearance was for a church picnic on the east side of Erie, and on paper it seemed simple enough. True, that side of town was not generally thought of as particularly secure, but it was a bright Sunday afternoon, so it seemed a reasonable enough request. Plus, the church seemed organized. There were small tents lining the open field, each staffed with volunteers overseeing some sort of game or craft for the families. Under a larger tent at one end of the park was Bible Bingo, and a baseball toss.

As I stepped into the heart of the activities, a screaming deluge of bodies came hurtling in my direction. Though some appeared traumatized by my appearance, other children of all ages and sizes pinned me down, pushing, pulling, punching, slapping, and grabbing at me. Predictably , their parents laughed as they documented the carnage.

I stooped to hug one kid and another leapt on my back, begging for a piggyback ride around the park. I shook him off. Another lifted up on the snout, causing the chin strap to dig into my neck, effectively choking me. I tried to pull away and winced as another one twisted the nose from side to side, wrenching my neck with it. But soon the initial wave of interest died down, and I thought I was about to be granted a reprieve. I was about to duck out for a quick breather when a sarcastic, pubescent voice rose from out of nowhere.

"Yo, Wolfman. Can I get a hug?"

I turned to see a skinny boy wearing a wifebeater and a straight brimmed baseball cap and I recognized him as one of the teens who'd been sitting outside the stink house.

Teenagers were probably the worst of all—especially the boys. Often, they sought to impress their friends, finding ways to harass me every chance they got. At the ballpark, though, this interaction was usually kept in check by the sizable police presence. If things got out of hand, a security guard or civic center police officer was on the spot, ready to diffuse the situation. During promotionals, however, I was on my own. As this kid engaged with me, I was faced with two options: 1) acknowledge him, give him a hug, and run the risk of him bopping me on the head or kicking me in the groin, or 2) ignore him; I could keep him at arm's length, but he and his friends would hang around like horseflies, waiting to bite at the first opportunity. And if they wanted to, there was nothing I could really do to stop them.

Figuring that it was best to get it over with, I opened my fuzz-covered arms for a half-hearted hug. He moved in and patted my shoulder jovially with his left arm. He muttered something under his breath that caused his friends to giggle. Just as I thought it was about to be over, he struck me fast and hard twice with what felt like the closed fist of his right hand just below my diaphragm, expelling the air from my lungs and leaving me heaving in a vain attempt to draw breath. He laughed and ran, his co-conspirators on his heels. They crossed the street and were gone before I felt my lungs expand again. As the physical panic of being unable to breathe passed, I did my best to draw slow, calming breaths, but my lungs ached and my heart pounded.

"Assholes," I groaned to myself.

Before I could find cover, another group of parents with kids cornered me and I found myself going through the motions, but something just didn't feel right. I was fatigued, but more so than I usually was, and I felt a little lightheaded. Soon, I noticed blood blooming on my side, saturating the artificial fur and baseball pinstripes. I knew then that kid had hit me with more than his fist. There must have been some sort of blade. Judging from the tear in my jersey, it was relatively small, but I couldn't tell how severe the actual wound was.

I clamped a paw over my side and shrugged off a few families on my way to the bingo tent. It was the busiest tent, packed with people, and I figured that was a good place to go looking for help.

In the tent, rows of people dabbed at their cards as a woman, admiring her nails, plucked a ping-pong ball from a cage and called out each of the letters and numbers.

"B-47," she said in a throaty whisper.

The players tapped furiously, marking the cards on the tables before them.

"Excuse me," I said, approaching a woman on the back bench. "But I need—"

"Shhh!"

I turned to a kind-looking man across the aisle.

"Excuse me."

"Shhh!" went the woman in the back row.

The old man looked up at me, then his eyes dropped to my side. "Oh, my Lord. You know you're bleedin'?"

Only then was I offered a seat and suitable place to remove my layers—first the thick uniform and fur-covered arms, and finally my bloody, sweat-soaked t-shirt. The wound itself was small, no more than a half-inch in length, but red oozed steadily through. From the crowd that gathered another woman, identifying herself as some kind of nurse, emerged with a small first aid kit. She snapped on a pair of latex gloves and extracted a gauze pad and small bottle of peroxide from the tiny case she carried.

First, she pulled the wound open and peered inside. Then poured the peroxide just above my wound. On contact, the clear liquid frothed and stung. She watched the bubbles pop for a while, then covered the wound with a gauze pad.

"Hold it there," she said, nodding at a fresh gauze pad she used to cover the cut. "Might need a stitch or two, but it don't look too bad."

I placed my hand over the pad and held it tightly against my skin. The cut burned and I felt some of the peroxide bubbles still popping in the wound.

At the local urgent care, a doctor examined me and shook her head.

"And what did they clean this with?" she asked.

"Peroxide, I think."

She gave a frustrated grunt and turned to a tray that held what looked like funky fish hooks, fine thread, and few pairs of pliers. "They're not supposed to do that. It damages the tissue." She proceeded to numb the area with a needle, then added, "Harder to stitch up. Takes longer to heal."

It was true that the wound wasn't that bad. Whatever I had been stuck with was small, like a box cutter or X-ACTO knife. Between C. Wolf's many layers—pinstriped baseball uniform, muscle suit, and the fur, I had barely been nicked by the tip of the blade.

Minor as the wound was, when I felt the pressure of the first suture tugging at my side, the realization of what had happened started to sink in. I had just been stabbed. I had been stabbed at a church picnic and the person who did it got away clean.

Questions immediately swirled in my head, but they weren't the questions common of true crime dramas on television where everyone is concerned with motive and means. No—instead my questions were more practical. Questions like, how do they bill this? Do they charge by the stitch? Will it be covered fully by workman's compensation or will I need to call my dad and have him bring me my insurance card?

Of all the questions, one seemed to echo the loudest in that moment—*is this worth it?*

That was the first time that question had ever been raised. It would not be the last.

Hound Dog

The instructions that had been handed to me were clear—pick up Elvis-style, rhinestone jumpsuit from an old lady named Viola. As I drove past the Millcreek Mall and across the overpass for I-79, I squinted down at the words scribbled just under the address.

"Look for a white house. Warning: Don't ask any questions or go into the garage. You'll never get out of there."

Curious, I continued on to where the road narrowed, rounded a bend, and spotted a silver mailbox with the house number I had been looking for. I eased my Lumina Z34 onto the concrete drive. The front bumper scraped the ground, and soon an old, heavyset woman with grizzled gray hair and a stern, pouchy face stepped outside her front door and onto the small landing. She glared down at me as I parked in front of her garage door on the same cracked-concrete pad as her own tarp-covered car. I climbed out, and she hobbled down the stairs to meet me.

"Yeah?" she asked in a harsh, throaty voice.

"Viola?" I asked.

"Don't know you."

"I'm Dan?" I said, my voice quiet and uneasy. I wondered then if anyone told her I'd be coming.

"So? I don't know you and I don't need whatever it is you're sellin'."

"I'm not," I said. "Rick sent me."

"Rick? Who's Rick?"

"Rick McGill? With the SeaWolves."

Until then, the old woman stood there, lips pressed tightly together, but at the sound of the word "SeaWolves" her face lifted. Her pouchy jowls pulled back into a parody of a smile, and her eyes widened, though the dark bags beneath them still asserted some gravity over the rest of her face.

"Oh," she gave a little chuckle. "Richard—what a deary. How is he?"

"Fine, I think," I answered, taken aback by the sudden shift in tone.

"Glad to hear," she said. "But why doesn't he come see me sometime instead of sending some lackey to come begging for a handout?"

I forced a smile and shrugged, trying not to take offense at the fact that I was, as she put it, just Rick's latest "lackey."

"Yeah, well." Viola turned and shuffled to the front of my car. "Guess I know what you came sniffin' around for."

She widened her stance and bent awkwardly at her waist, gripping the handle of the garage door with one hand, bracing herself against the bumper of my car with the other. Then, with a strength of which I would not have thought her capable, she heaved the door open with a single pull. The door's stubborn, rusted wheels screamed on their tracks, some clearly refusing to roll at all, as the door slammed to a stop against the ceiling. With the contents revealed, I felt a shiver running the length of my spine and I took an uneasy step back.

The dead eyes of something like Dora (the Explorer) were the first to catch my gaze. Her decapitated head sat on a makeshift table—a piece of plywood perched on a pair of homemade sawhorses. Poor Dora's nose was missing, and in its place was a split seam, spilling the cotton batting that Viola had been using to give Dora her shape. Along the walls, heads peered down from shelves, their corresponding body parts severed and peeking out of the milk crates beneath them. It was the garage of Norman Bates, if his taxidermy hobby had moved from roadkill to cartoon characters. Many appeared to be akin to characters that I had known as a child—Snoopy, Woodstock, Garfield; but others were so grotesquely deformed that they were impossible to place—a large green alligator, a yellow duck, and a faceless, nameless approximation of a mouse.

Viola shuffled past the heads to the back wall. There were coat racks there, slung with garment bags and feather boas. She flicked through each, glancing at the masking tape that identified its contents before shuffling on to the next one.

"You—uh—not Rick," she called to me over her shoulder. "You're the one who will be wearing this?"

The sound of her voice made me jump, diverting my attention from some sort of anthropomorphic amoeba. Then, registering what she had asked, I nodded.

"Come over here then so we can get your size."

Overwhelmed, my eyes roved again over the contents of that space. Then, Rick's warning slipped from my mind, and I followed her further inside.

The smell of sawdust tickled my nostrils, and I sneezed several times in quick succession. Viola continued sifting through the garment bags without so much as an obligatory "bless you."

Up close, the characters that lined the walls were well worn, with matted, balding fur. Their bright colors were dimmed by dust and dirt. Fresh stitches and patchwork made the repaired spots pop, even in the dim light of the yellow incandescent bulbs.

The old woman eyed me as I drew closer to her.

"You're about a '62, I think."

I blinked. "No," I said, offended by her gross miscalculation. "I mean, I have about a thirty-inch waist."

"Yeah," she nodded. "Just as I thought. You're about the build he was back when he was coming out the army."

She pulled a bag from the coat rack and handed it to me. A sticker on the outside read "The King, 1962-1965."

"This one should work," she said. "You want to try it on?"

"No, thanks," I said, remembering the advice on Rick's note and realizing that I was now well into the danger zone. "If you think it'll work, I'll take your word for it."

"Should be fine," she said, turning to survey her life's work. "So, you like them?"

She beamed proudly at the shelves.

"Yeah," I said. "They're something."

"Took me years, but now it's a nice little business."

"Yeah?"

"Sure. Didn't you ever wonder who made all those costumes around town?"

"Not really," I said. "I guess I just assumed someone from out of town."

"You'd think that, but nope. C. Wolf, Shooter, the Smiths hot dogs," she said. "All mine. I started as a hobby. Years later, I built a little empire—one piece at a time."

"And what about all these?"

107

"Rentals mostly," she said. "For parties and birthdays."

"Well, they look—great. Really cool."

I tucked the bag under my arm and started out of the open garage door when I heard Viola's voice echo behind me.

"Before you go, would you mind helping me with something?"

"I've really gotta get back," I said. "I have a game tonight."

"Yeah, but not until 7:00," she said. "You've got about three hours and this won't take too long."

I'm not sure exactly how it happened, but the next thing I knew, strips of felt-like, fleshy-colored fabric were being wrapped and straight-pinned around my arms and legs as Viola began piecing together the body of what I assumed would be Dora, in what would clearly be her latest violation of international copyright and trademark law.

***

By the time I got back to the ballpark, the gates were already open. The corporate suites were sold out and were owed a visit from C. Wolf. I didn't have much time to make the usual pregame visits. That didn't stop Rick from ribbing me a bit when I got back to the stadium. He pushed himself up from his desk as I passed his office on my way to the prop room. He chuckled as I hung the garment bag on the wire shelves and unzipped it to reveal the white jumpsuit.

"She got you inside, didn't she?" Rick asked.

I looked over my shoulder, wide-eyed, and blinked a few times. There was no need for words.

"I warned you," he sighed. "Last time I was there, she showed me damn near every costume she ever made. Still, it's here—you're here—and Hound Dog is up for the top of the third. We'll have one of the girls bring the mic stand down to the third base dugout. If it goes well, have an encore ready for the top of the fifth on the first base side."

***

Clamoring up onto the third base dugout, I felt unusually cool for this stage of the game—temperature-wise anyway. I wore the usual furry gloves and the scraggly, oversized head, but my torso and legs were covered in the thin, airy material that felt so much better than C. Wolf's full uniform. The suit clung and moved, as if it were tailor-made just for me. I suppose Viola had a pretty good eye for sizes after all these years. A diamond girl slid a disconnected mic and stand up to me, and as she did so I remembered that scene from the movie *Forrest Gump*, when the young hero in leg braces met Elvis in his mother's boardinghouse. The young musician sat on his bed playing the guitar while Forrest showed him how he swung his hips to the beat of the song "Hound Dog." When the song finally played over the PA system, I did my best young Forrest impression for the crowd.

The combined performances had me in the jumpsuit for a grand total of four minutes, and the payoff hardly seemed worth the three-hour ordeal of picking up the damn thing. So, instead of waiting for daylight to return the jumpsuit, I drove directly to Viola's house after the game, opened her front storm door, and hung the garment bag's hanger over the top of the door. I closed it softly, so as to not risk waking her, and I left it there with a note and a printed photo of C. Wolf in the suit, dancing to "Hound Dog" in front of a crowd that barely noticed.

Dating Hazards

Unless you were one of the popular kids in high school, dating was probably about as fun as leaping from the high-dive platform and diving head-first into a swimming pool filled with thumbtacks. First, you let down your guard, bear your insecurities, and when you're all exposed and at your most vulnerable, the object of your affection—well—they just cut you. Sometimes the rejection will come quickly and the wounds are superficial—that is, if you're lucky. But mostly you're not. Most of the time, they drag it out. The longer they do, the farther the fall, and the deeper those thumbtacks will dig in.

High school was tough enough, but when I got to college, things took a turn from bad to the impossible. Every day there were young, attractive women around me—but my presence never seemed to grab their attention. When my friends wanted to date someone new, they often relied on their jobs. Whether stocking the T-shirt wall at Hot Topic, slathering mayo on footlongs at Subway, or fetching cross-trainers for women at the local sporting goods store, most of my soon-to-be married friends met their future spouses while working at their college jobs. Unfortunately, that was never an option for me. When working as a mascot, you quickly learn to never date the people you meet on the job.

Don't get me wrong, I've met a lot of people in this line of work, and many were great. Some were intrigued by the mystique of the mask, but when you consider exactly what you're doing, the dating hazards are readily apparent. I mean, you're basically working all year as a giant stuffed animal and there are only a few types of people who would consider that sort of thing appealing. As obvious as the challenges posed by these dating demographics were, it was the obscure dangers you had to watch out for. And the most notable that I ever discovered was named Ceana.

We've met Ceana before, back in Altoona. She was helping us to organize the Make-A-Wish event we did early in the 2004 season. She was that beautiful blonde who had worked with the Curve for a while, the one who once confessed to me that she "was a wolf too." When she first revealed this to me, I had no real understanding of what this actually meant. It wasn't until I met her at the ballpark in Erie a month or two later that I became a bit more educated on the subject.

When I met Ceana for the second time, I had been playing with two toddlers—Jen and Ben—who came to nearly every game with their parents. They sat along the railing in the reserved seating behind home plate, and every time I passed by the kids laughed and called to me. Given that they were regulars, I'd always take the time to stop, at least for a minute or two. I reached through the railing, allowed each of the kids to slap me a solid high-five, and then I spread out the fingers on both of my fuzzy paws and pretended to get them stuck between vertical rungs. First, Ben freed one paw. Then, just as Jen turned my opposite paw sideways to thread it back through, my free paw would become wedged between another set of rungs. We repeated this procedure several times, and it never seemed to get old. But on one occasion, just as Ben and Jen freed my paws for a third time, I heard another voice calling to me from higher up.

"Hey, C. Wolf!"

I looked up into the stands. Seated high in the reserved seating, just below the private boxes, was a familiar woman with long, blonde curls. She had a natural tan and her hair appeared to be wet. Stunning as she was, though, she was not alone. There was another woman sitting beside her who was every bit her double. The first woman waved as if she knew me and gestured for me to climb up their way. So, when I had finished teasing the kids, I turned up the stairs and wandered in her direction.

"Remember me?" Ceana asked, as I slid into an empty seat in the row ahead of her.

I cocked my head to the side in the same manner that a curious puppy might. She was familiar, though I couldn't quite place where I knew her from."

"It's Ceana," she chortled. "From Altoona?"

"Ahhh," I growled in C. Wolf's voice. "That's right. How could I forget?"

She turned then, motioning to the younger woman beside her. "This is my little sister, Theresa."

I extended my paw and Theresa shook it enthusiastically.

"Call me Tee," she said. "Everyone does."

"So, Ceana and Tee, what brought you guys up from Altoona?"

"Oh, I'm just up visiting my folks," Ceana explained.

"We grew up in Erie," Tee chimed in.

Ceana had mentioned something about that, but until then it had slipped my mind.

"I went to Behrend, but transferred to main campus for my last year. Tee's in her second year at Behrend now."

"Yeah," Tee said. "Only I chose a real major."

"Whatever," Ceana scoffed. "You play with computers while I hang out with the athletic guys all day. Which career sounds more fun?" She nodded to me then. "Am I right, C. Wolf?"

I nodded, thoughtfully. "Your sister has a point, you know. I mean, she gets to hang out with people like me and— let's face it—we can be a lot of fun."

"Yeah," said Tee. A knowing grin split her face and she tossed her sister a sideways glance. "My sister tells me all about that sort of 'fun.' But hey, whatever it takes. I don't judge."

Ceana blushed slightly and shushed her sister.

"What?" Tee said. "I thought you said he already knew?"

Flustered, Ceana's face reddened further, something she attempted to hide behind the cover of her program. Curiously, I cocked my head to the side once more, glancing back and forth between the two sisters.

"Too much?" Tee asked.

Ceana squirmed and her face chameleoned through three distinct shades of pink.

"What? You said you told him when he came down to Altoona."

"Told me what?"

Tee fixed me with a mischievous smirk, one of her pencil-thin eyebrows raised. "That she's a wolf. And she likes other wolves." She paused, considered her sister, and then mock whispered in my direction, "It's kind of her thing."

113

"Ah," I said. "I get it."

I didn't.

Yes, Ceana had previously let slip that she considered herself "a wolf too." And judging from the way that she was cowering in the seat beside her sister, I began to gather that Ceana was more than a little embarrassed by her sister conveying that information. Judging by the way Ceana squirmed in her seat and by my analysis of the heavy-handed clues that "Ceana liked wolves" and the fact that I was currently dressed as one, I eventually concluded that she had more than a professional interest in *me*. Needless to say, I was flattered. It wasn't every day that someone like her showed an interest in a mildly awkward guy with self-esteem issues. I looked at her, excitement swelling inside me at the prospect of a date with Ceana, but I played it cool, aided exceptionally well by the fact that this giant wolf's head shielded my own obscene grin from view.

"So," I began, focusing my attention squarely on Tee as I spoke, "if I'm picking up what you're putting down, you're suggesting that if a certain 'wolf' expressed an interest in the other 'wolf' that these two 'wolves' might really hit it off?"

By this point, Ceana had pulled a knee to her chest and she was trying, desperately, to make herself as small as possible. Tee, on the other hand, grinned a broad grin as she turned and smacked her sister hard on the shoulder.

"See, I told you! And you were afraid he wouldn't be interested."

Ceana rubbed at her shoulder and peered out from behind the program, a little apprehensively. I stood, stepped over the seat, and knelt beside Ceana, as Tee grinned stupidly at her sister. I reached out with two paws and took Ceana's hand into mine. Still pink in the face, Ceana sat up, her feet sliding from the seat. She smiled weakly, considering me out of the corner of her eye.

"Ms. Ceana," I began, in a parody of a wedding proposal. "Would you mind if this old wolf would buy you dinner tomorrow night?"

"Aww," Tee mocked. "He's so romantic."

Shielding her face with her free hand, Ceana shushed and scolded her, though she too was fighting back an exuberant grin. Tee raised her hands in apparent surrender.

"Well...," Ceana bit her lip, as she regained her composure, her color returning to normal. "...could we stay in?"

***

She greeted me at the door in an off-the-shoulder top that displayed a black bra strap. A matching lace choker was slung around her thin neck, displaying a silver medallion. Over her opposite shoulder, her hair had been tamed and draped. The dimmed apartment lights that bathed the room behind her illuminated her head like a halo. I smiled at her, but Ceana looked coyly away.

"Come in," she said.

Ceana stepped to the side and I brushed lightly against her as I crossed the threshold. She sniffed slightly as I passed and I thought that she must have liked the new deodorant that I had switched to.

The apartment was nice, a new construction not far from Penn State's Erie campus. It was where Ceana had started her degree and where her sister was currently attending. The carpet was beige, the walls were white. There were a few pictures hanging about a large, great room. On one end of the space was a kitchen, separated from the living room by a long island and dining area. The table was set for two—two white plates and two white bowls sitting on saucers and a cinnamon scented Yankee candle was placed in the space between them.

On the wall opposite the kitchen, a flatscreen television was mounted and angled slightly toward the sitting area that contained a couch and two chairs.

"Dinner will be ready in a bit," Ceana said, ducking behind the kitchen island to retrieve something from the cupboard there. "Take a seat in the living room, if you'd like."

I settled at the end of the couch, where I could observe Ceana moving about the kitchen. A plume of steam rose as she pulled the lid off a pot and stirred the contents.

"So, this is your sister's place?" I asked.

"Yep," Ceana said. "She has some roommates, but they're gone for most of the summer so she's got the run of the place."

"Ah. So, when can we expect her back?"

She flashed a seductive smile. "Sometime tomorrow. Tee said she'd was going to stay at Mom's tonight. You know."

The implications of this made my stomach flutter.

I had just turned twenty-one and never before had I been on a date where someone was so forward. Rarely, people had flirted with me on occasion, but I was usually only aware of this after the fact, when the opportune moment had passed. I was painfully naïve when it came to dating, so the prospect of having an entire apartment to ourselves was equal parts nerve-wracking and exhilarating. Where would this night go? I didn't know, but I hoped that Ceana and I would discover that together.

When dinner was served, she scooped a mix of chicken, rice, and stir-fried vegetables into the bowls on the table and lit the candle on the table between us.

"It's the best I could do on such short notice," she said, adjusting the dimmer switch on the wall, until the warm glow of the apartment was replaced by the flickering flame of the candle.

Overall, the effect was visually stunning. Her pale eyes appeared almost iridescent, and the shadows flickered across the flattering contours of her face. A wide, Cheshire grin was firmly in place, and something about the lighting had a slimming effect on her exposed teeth. As I occupied the chair at the table across from her, Ceana's smile morphed into something more like a sneer, amplifying the prominence of her long-pointed cuspids. I was startled then, not by her beauty—though she certainly was beautiful—but by the way she seemed to be displaying those teeth. She stared, hungrily up at me from across the table, almost as if to remind me that, human as she was, with teeth like those, she was a predator and she was on the prowl.

My stomach went queasy then—though whether this was from a resurgence of date-night nerves or the incompatibility of the mingled aromas of boiled chicken and cinnamon that was now filling the room, I could not be sure.

"Well?" Ceana said, her nostrils flared, drawing in a deep breath.

I sniffed.

"Smells good," I lied, only then realizing that the table set before us had no silverware.

Ceana lowered her face over her bowl, her eyes maintaining their lock on me, and she certainly appeared quite wolf-like. Then, without warning, she opened her mouth and plunged, face-first, into her own bowl.

What the fuck! I thought to myself, though I said nothing. Instead, I watched her ravenously chomping and chewing and licking her lips between bites. With each mouthful, she dug deeper into her dish. I could only stare. The mess of rice was now spilling onto the table and floor around her. I watched it fall and for a split second I thought, *what about her sister's security deposit?* Then I looked up and remembered, *there is a woman sitting across from me with her face buried in her food.* Then I considered my own dish.

It shows what my dating prospects were like just then, given that I did not run screaming from that apartment the moment she started eating. Instead, I thought, *beautiful girl, questionable table manners; I can work with this.* So, I followed her lead, tentatively lowering my own face over the bowl in front of me. With my front teeth, I fished out a pale strip of cooked chicken from the rice, threw my head back, and allowed it to drop into my mouth. I chewed.

The food was bland; there was no salt or seasoning, no soy sauce or dressing. When I extracted a mouthful of vegetables, they tasted as if they had been sautéed in burnt butter. Still, I didn't want to be rude. After all, she did warn me that she "was a wolf," and I was now just beginning to realize what she must have meant by that. So, I ate what I could, but when Ceana had finished lapping up some water from the bowl beside her main course, I leaned back from my meal as well.

The table and carpet were a mess, as was Ceana herself. Her once neat hair seemed wilder then, as it was inundated with flecks of rice and even some fragments of carrot and snow pea. Her face appeared wet, possibly from her own saliva, as her tongue kept licking her lips full-circle while she stared at me.

"That was great," I said.

I leaned back in my chair and stretched.

Without warning, she gave a little snort and leapt to the ground. A little unnerved at this point, I jumped up from my chair. Ceana's arms were stretched out. Her hips tested the limits of the tight, low-rise jeans she was wearing. Her body's position reminded me of the puppies we had when I was a kid, bowing in the way that they do to beckon others to play. I stammered, attempting to gather my thoughts.

"I—uh—"

Ceana gave a little hop and her shirt slid up her back, slightly, revealing the purple and blue of a tattoo—the silhouette of a wolf, howling in front of a full moon. The sight of the tattoo placated my panic momentarily. I looked past the wolfish Ceana posturing on the floor, and tried to focus on the rather well-dressed, blonde and the privacy of an apartment that we would have to ourselves for the rest of the evening.

I considered the situation and my 21-year old lizard brain thought, *beautiful girl, questionable table manners, but enthusiastic; I can work with this.* So I dropped to the floor and bowed back. She smiled then, and I felt my own face flush. She snapped her teeth, then pounced. She tackled me. We fell back together and rolled onto our sides. We lay there on the floor and my pulse quickened. I thought that she was about to kiss me. Instead, she opened her mouth as wide as her jaws would permit and proceeded to press her teeth against my still mostly closed mouth. She nodded until I realized that she wanted me to do the same. I opened my mouth and her teeth connected with my own.

I thought, *beautiful girl, questionable table manners, enthusiastic, who is now trying to eat my face; I think can work with this.*

She wrapped her arms around me and, following her lead, I rolled with her about the floor, our teeth clicking awkwardly against one another. It was almost as if she were

119

trying to force my jaws closed with her own and I wondered, *is this some kind of a wolf thing?*

After a few minutes she rolled me over, and I felt her full weight pressing down on top of me. She placed her hands on my chest and pushed herself up, resting her full weight on my sternum. As she did so, I could read, for the first time, a name engraved on the silver tag displayed on the silver medallion that hung from her lace choker. *Wylla Wolfson.*

"What's that?" I asked.

"Oh—I think you know what it is," she said.

Ceana rocked back and I felt her legs gripping my hips. My face went hot.

"Not that," I said, distracted. I nodded toward her neck and tried to calm my nerves.

She reached one hand up and grabbed the medallion. "You mean this?"

I nodded.

She giggled. "It's just my name."

"I thought your name was Ceana."

"It is—sort of," Ceana said. Then, in response to my expression, she continued. "My mom named me Ceana. Wylla is my preferred name—my *fursona.*"

"Your fursona?" I repeated. Never having heard the term before, I thought I had misunderstood her.

"Yeah. For conventions, mostly," she said. Then, leaning in, she nibbled my ear again and whispered, "And for other things."

"Oh," I said. Distracted by the sensation of her full weight on top of me, I feigned comprehension, a little nervous, but still eager to see where things were headed.

She paused then, still straddling me, and pushed herself up again. She appeared to be trying to decide something. Then she finally asked, "You wouldn't want to see, would you ?"

Failing to see how the answer to that question could possibly go wrong, I blurted out the only word that came to mind. "Yes."

She rolled off me and turned in the direction of the bedroom door. I perked up, thinking that she might want me to follow her, but no such luck. Instead, she glanced over her shoulder in the doorway, grinned, then slipped inside the bedroom, pushing the door shut behind her.

Unsure of what I should do, I stood and leaned against the arm of the couch, trying to appear cooler than I obviously was. When the door finally swung open, it took a little time for me to register exactly what I was seeing.

She stood in the doorway, wearing a black lace teddy that barely concealed a voluptuous body. That lingerie hugged curves that I didn't expect, and the seductive material was overtaxed, barely concealing her curvaceous, soft, hairy body.

Ceana was covered, head-to-toe, by thick gray fur and she had a tail, which had been threaded carefully through a hole in her lace. Sure, she still had blue eyes, but now they were the size of baseballs and were positioned, unblinking, atop a foot-long, cartoon muzzle.

My mind was pure panic as she pushed me onto the couch and crawled back on top of me.

Suddenly that deductive voice in my head reasserted itself—*beautiful girl, questionable table manners, enthusiastic, tried eating my face—that happens—but holy hell, she's dressed like a wolf. No worries, I can—I can—I cannot work with this.*

My muscles tensed and Ceana seemed to realize that her costume was not having the desired effect on me. She then

121

suggested the only thing that she thought might help to get her evening back on track.

"Maybe you just need to go get C. Wolf?"

Only then did I *fully* realize what she had meant by "I'm a wolf too." I had heard whispers, rumors mainly, of the "furry fandom community." Every now and again, when someone found out about my job, they'd ask if I'd ever encountered "a furry." Until then, I hadn't—not that I knew of anyway.

"I think it's getting late," I said. "And we've had a long homestand. Plus, C. Wolf is definitely in need of a good cleaning. The smell alone, that would just ruin the mood."

"I get it," she said, pulling off Wylla's head and looking a little sullen. "I suppose it's a little different when you end up doing this for a job." We sat side-by-side on the couch. "This is supposed to be fun. It should never feel like work."

"Yeah, I suppose it shouldn't," I said, wondering if she was referring to just the costumes.

I felt guilty, as though I had led her on. Although she was clearly disappointed, Ceana was kind in the wake of my rejection. We sat there for a while, talking about Wylla Wolfson, and she opened up about her experience with the furry community. She described the release that she felt, just being Wylla sometimes, but there was also a lot of frustration. The furry community was extremely complex. For some, it was a social outlet. They simply enjoyed the cosplay. It was only for a very small subset of the furry community that there was any romantic or sexual dimension to their fursonas at all, but for someone who identified as a straight, cis female, the options appeared even more limited. The final nail in the coffin of Wylla Wolfson's love life was her belief that the fursona of any potential lovers had to be compatible—wolves with wolves, rabbits with rabbits, cats with cats.

I listened to her talk for a while. As she shared all of these personal details, there was a part of me that wanted to hug her. A part that seemed to say, "Screw it. Put that head on and let's try this again," but I knew it was a nonstarter. When it comes to romance, there are some things that you can work with, limits you might be willing to push, but I had inadvertently found some invisible boundary that I had never considered and I knew then that it was best to just move on.

I had known rejection in my life, but I had never been on this end of it. As Ceana shuffled back into the bedroom, I could see some of myself in the way she moved. Her slumped shoulders, eyes fixed on the floor. When she came out wearing the same outfit that she had worn over dinner, she looked as if she had been crying. I knew what she was feeling and believed—rightly or wrongly—that the best thing was to cut our evening short.

We lingered on the doorstep for a moment, the awkwardness of our goodbye hanging in the air like the ghosts of every bad date that I had ever been on. Finally, I opened my arms and invited her in for a hug. She leaned into me and I tried to say through that simple action that I was sorry. She squeezed me back, as if today that she wished it could have gone differently—that the night could have been something to remember.

I guess it was.

Finding Love

As we have already established in the previous chapter, there are many reasons that you should never date the people you meet on the job. On the other hand, should you happen to meet someone elsewhere and you believe that there is any potential for a positive long-term relationship, you should bring them to work with you, at least once. If they accept the invitation, one of two things will occur: either the experience will bond you together so completely that, in just a few years' time, you'll marry, move across the country, and have children in some random town in the American Middle West; or the experience will be so unpleasant that it will dissolve any respect that they ever had for you, causing your relationship to devolve into a fiery ball so spectacular that even Michael Bay would blush at the sight of it.

Early in my first season with the SeaWolves, when I was still dually employed with the Otters, I ran into a slight predicament. Channellock was announcing a major sponsorship of the mascots for both the Otters and SeaWolves. This was an exciting development, given that a portion of this sponsorship money would fund upgrades to the costumes, as well as key operational expenses. There was a bit of a catch, though. Both mascots were required to attend a major press event, at Conneaut Lake Park, where the company would make a formal announcement and present the funds, in the form of a giant check, to both Shooter and C. Wolf in person. Because of this, I found myself double booked—two suits, one body.

I had few contacts whom I felt would be a good fit. Rodger, one of my oldest friends, was a bit of a thespian. He acted at a local dinner theater, starred in a few noteworthy productions in the region, and had hobbies, like civil war reenacting, that required him to regularly adopt different personas. He was talented and fun, so naturally I thought him a good fit, but when I called him to see if he'd be able to give me a hand, his reaction was a little less than enthusiastic.

"Sorry, buddy," he said, not really sounding sorry at all.

"Come on, it's a quick $25 for ten minutes," I argued.

"Yeah," he groaned. "The thing is—it's not going to happen."

I made a few more calls, and each response was less enthusiastic than the one before. Running low on options, I did the only thing I could reasonably think of—I called Renee, a girl I had recently made the acquaintance of at college. She was a free-spirited, undeclared major with blonde dreads who loved incense and reggae—and everything that went with it. We had been "hanging out" and seemed to be having fun when the gig was booked. We had gone to a few dollar movies at the Millcreek Mall and had eaten lunch together almost every day during that previous term.

Neither of us had ever been to Conneaut Lake Park before. It had one of the oldest wooden roller coasters in the United States—the Blue Streak—and the Devil's Den was legendary among theme-park enthusiasts. The idea occurred to me that we could make a date of it. Maybe I could take her to help me out with the mascots. It'd be a quick 20 minutes, in and out. Then we could hang out and ride some rides, play some games, and see if there was any chemistry there. It seemed benign enough. We'd have free park entry and complimentary rides all in exchange for spending 20 minutes in a costume. Given that Renee was one of the most carefree people I had ever met in my life at that point—what could possibly go wrong?

So, I made the call.

"Hey, Renee? Are you free on Saturday?"

"Oh—yeah. Why do you ask?"

"I'm in a jam and I need some help with something."

"Alright," she answered readily. "What is it?"

"Channellock is making an announcement on Saturday and I need to have both C. Wolf and Shooter down in Conneaut Lake for it," I said, not really considering my audience. "But there's only one of me and I could really use two of me."

"I can see how that'd be a problem," she said.

"Well, yeah. So, I was wondering—would you want to help me out and wear one of the suits? It's a quick twenty-minute thing. In and out."

She paused a moment and then answered with, "Question. What the hell is a Channellock?"

"Oh. They make tools—wrenches. They're announcing a sponsorship with both teams. It's kind of this big thing."

"I see. So, you're stuck then? No options?"

"Pretty much," I said, adding, "and there's a quick $25 in it for you. Plus, we can hang out after if you'd like."

She hesitated.

"And you'll owe me?"

"Definitely," I agreed.

"In that case, sure."

When Saturday came, I picked Renee up from her apartment off campus and we made the drive together down to Conneaut Lake. In the parking lot, I pulled the two costumes out of the trunk of my car.

"So, which one do you want to be?" I asked. "Your choice."

She considered both of the bags carefully, opening one oversized duffle, then the other.

"Um, the wolf," she said, looking a little disappointed.

"All right," I said, then out of curiosity I asked, "Why that one?"

"Because, the baseball season has just started and you've clearly had less time to funk this one up."

She had a point. Although Shooter had been recently laundered at the end of the hockey season, the bag's fabric was still inundated with several seasons of stale sweat. The maroon and blue bag that held C. Wolf, on the other hand, had been sanitized in the off-season so that when it was opened, the reassuring scent of clean was all that rose up to greet you.

We changed in the parking lot behind my car. We each slipped into character before we even entered the park. Conneaut Lake Park had had a tumultuous decade, occasionally remaining closed for entire summers, so there was a bit of a buzz about it when it was poised to open that year. The gates were open to visitors as were the picnic grounds. A few of the smaller rides were running, though the big draws (including The Bluestreak coaster and The Devil's Den) were shuttered, I assume pending repairs. Still, a reasonably large crowd was present as we wandered past the main concourse,

127

until one of the workers finally indicated the picnic structure where we were supposed to be.

Along the way, Renee seemed to take to the job well enough. When the kids found us, she stooped down onto one knee and wrapped her arms around them, and I noticed her dreads in a tangled ponytail peeking out from the base of C. Wolf's head. When we found our way to the pavilion, Renee strutted naturally up to the side of the president of Channellock, who posed with two massive checks, made out to each of the teams. He made the announcement in front of his employees as members of the press from Erie and Meadville snapped photos of the exchange. Once the press got what they needed, we worked the room, greeting and posing for photographs with employees. Beer had been flowing for a bit before we arrived, and when it became evident that a few of the employees in attendance had been overserved, Renee and I made sure to stick close together. Our instincts were that there were safety in numbers.

As we moved about the pavilion, a group of picnickers began to get handsy. A cluster of middle-aged women groped at me when we slid past them and I heard one sneer something that sounded like, "Hey, you ain't C. Wolf. You're a she-wolf."

I turned and saw the woman reach up and give Renee's exposed hair a little tug. C. Wolf's head jerked suddenly and I knew from the way that Renee staggered that it must have hurt. That was my cue to get her out of there. I took C. Wolf's paw and led the way out into the daylight.

Less than thirty minutes after we arrived at the park, we were back at the car, peeling off the pelts and tucking them back into the bags from which they came. But as soon as Renee was clear from the suit, I could tell something in her demeanor had changed. Usually happy and easygoing, she lowered herself into the passenger seat of my car, her expression stern and irritated. I stuffed the mascots into the trunk and climbed behind the wheel.

"You alright?" I asked.

Renee didn't respond. She simply turned away, gazing out the passenger window. I knew then that it probably wasn't a good idea to go back into the park and take advantage of our free ride passes. I slid the key into the ignition and the engine turned over.

"What's wrong?" I asked again.

"Let's just go," she said simply.

I backed the car out of the space and headed back toward Edinboro. We were driving past campus before she finally broke her silence.

"Is it always like that?" she asked.

"Like what?"

"Back there," she said. "Do they always grab at you like that?"

I shrugged. "Sometimes. They serve a lot of beer at games. People tend to lose track of personal boundaries at that point."

"But you just walked on. It was like you didn't even care."

"What do you mean? As soon as I saw them pull your hair, I left."

"Not that," she muttered. "Could care less about my hair. It's what they did to you."

"What?" I said, a little confused.

"Those bitches," she spat. "Grabbing at your ass like that. That's—like—sexual assault."

"Oh," I said, a little embarrassed. "I guess I got used to it. Kind of part of the job."

"No," she countered, "it damn well isn't. At least, it shouldn't be."

It was the first time—and last time—I had ever heard her raise her voice. She was still seething, continuing to vent and shake her head as we arrived outside her apartment.

"Sorry," she finally said, drawing long, deep breaths in an attempt to calm herself. "It's just—I know what it's like for people to brush up against you, like you don't have a say about it."

"Oh," I said, understanding then that she must have had some sort of history of which I had been previously unaware.

I was surprised, but I guess I shouldn't have been. I mean I knew college guys often lacked tact and courtesy, but I liked Renee and the thought of random men touching on her was upsetting. Even though I had never thought twice about someone grabbing on me while I was in C. Wolf, I did understand why it could be upsetting for her.

"Yeah," she continued. "But that makes what they were doing to you all the worse."

"I'm not sure I follow."

"It's guys—I just kind of expect it of them. But to see women doing it, they should fucking know better."

At the time, her comment didn't quite compute. It was an odd double standard, almost as if she had become so desensitized to the behavior of men, she had simply come to dismiss it as part of their nature. For her, women should have known what it's like to be objectified and, for that reason if no other, should have taken care not to do it.

Put off by what I had come to expect as a normal occupational hazard, I did my best to empathize with her and attempted to change the subject to a more enjoyable prospect of doing something together that afternoon.

"Sorry," she said. "That suit made me feel a little gross. Think I'm just going to go shower. I'll call you later, though."

I tried not to let on how disappointed I was. With a quick hug in the car, Renee opened her door and walked up the sidewalk to the entrance of the building.

Any prospective relationship that we might have considered fizzled fast after that.

***

The next time a young woman donned a mascot suit with me, it was a gorgeous young lady named Emmy. And as you might have guessed by this point, the end result was considerably different.

I met Emmy on December 17, 2004, during winter break. Naturally athletic, she was a first-year college student who ran track and cross country for Slippery Rock University. She had a shoulder-length perm of wavy locks that looked quite natural, and though I was immediately struck by her high cheekbones and gray-blue eyes, these were not the first attributes that initially caught my attention. No. It was the cardboard sign that she had stapled to the back of her shirt.

At the time, she was working at one of the local Taco Bells with some mutual friends. She was jamming out behind the counter with her back to me. The cardboard sign she wore displayed the message "it's hip to be square." The words were scribbled in black permanent marker and I can only assume that she did so ironically, given that the cardboard was more rectangular than square, and she would turn out to be the smartest person that I'd ever met. She danced confidently; her shoulders and hips popped and shimmied to the music. Bonny and bold, she demonstrated more confidence than I ever had performing as any mascot. It lived in her Scottish skin; no mask, no mystery required.

Emmy never intended to date me at the time, but at the prompting of our friends, she agreed to go out with me one night, despite her apparent reservation. Even after she agreed to "hang out," she made her boundaries clear; I was not to expect this to turn into anything like a relationship. She assured me that the moment I did, this whole thing would be over.

"I'm not looking for anything, really," she said. "We're just hanging out over break while I'm bored. When I go back to school, I'm gone and that's it."

Clearly, this was intended to be a short-term deal, and it wasn't entirely unexpected. At the time, I was still struggling with low self-esteem and I knew instinctively that I was not Emmy's type. I even made the mistake of telling her so.

"That's fine," I said, pretending to be cool with the arrangement. Then I added "You're way out of my league anyway."

"What the fuck does that mean?"

In my effort to be "cool" about our arrangement, I had clearly said the wrong thing. Her eyes flashed dangerously.

"What the fuck do you mean, league? There are no leagues. You think that way and we can just end this now."

I shut up. In my defense, though she was (and still is) the most impressive person I've ever met. One semester into school and she had a 4.0 GPA, while after three years, I was only able to wrestle mine up to an embarrassing 2.9. She was a real athlete who was still competing with a team, and though I was in decent shape and working in the Minor Leagues, I was little more than a talisman or lucky charm. The only things I had going for me were good personal references from our shared acquaintances and a car.

Over the next several weeks, we hung out—as per our arrangement. We ate out a few times, went to some movies, and generally seemed to be having a good time, but soon winter break was over, and so was our time together.

It was then that Emmy asked for a final favor.

"I have an indoor track meet next weekend," she said. "And I could really use a ride back to school."

"Yeah. No problem," I said, adding, "Maybe I'll stick around to watch you run or something."

On the day of the meet, I settled into a spot near the track's inside lane and watched Emmy warm up and stretch with a few of her teammates. They giggled to themselves and I noticed a few of them glancing in my direction.

"And who's he?" I heard one of the girls ask. "Is he here to see you?"

Emmy glanced over her shoulder with a cherubic smirk. Then without any warning, she shouted across the track to me. "Hey, Dan. You want to start dating?"

Given the established terms and conditions she presented me with over winter break, the question was confusing to say the least. Yes, I welcomed the development. I had been single for a while and was really interested in exploring something with Emmy, but she had been very clear—she was not looking for anything. There was a sort of gut check then, and a voice inside goaded me on.

"Sure," I said. "If you want."

Emmy grinned and turned back to her teammates. "Well, I guess he's with me, now."

When the meet was over and we were alone, I walked Emmy back to her dorm and asked her what had changed.

"Nothing really," she said. "It's just dating. It's not like we're talking marriage or anything."

"Oh," I thought, a little disappointed. "So still, nothing serious here?"

"God no," she chuckled to herself. "You're an English major. I couldn't possibly marry an English major."

"Well, why date then?"

Emmy shrugged. "Why not?"

Six months later we had safely progressed beyond "hanging out." I had started my second baseball season with the SeaWolves, and Emmy had taken a summer job, running rides at Waldemere, the local amusement park. We talked every day and saw each other as often as we could. Usually after games, I'd shower and rush across the Bayfront Connector and pick her up when the park closed.

We bonded quickly over our experiences. Both of us had some tumult on the home fronts—tension with parents and siblings, support structures that we had relied upon either failing or going through a period of restructuring. Needless to say, when we needed something, the person we came to rely on most to get through it was each other.

Although Emmy greatly improved my personal outlook on life, one day, in early June, I once again found myself in the need of help on the professional side of things. Needless to say, my options were a little thin and I was about to ask her for a huge favor—one that seemed to have destroyed any chance that I had with Renee almost exactly one year earlier.

Every June, the team organized a party for C. Wolf's birthday, which took place during the first Sunday home game of that month. When the tradition began, it took the form of a simple mascot mania, where costume characters from around the city converged on Jerry Uht Park and participated in a series of challenges and activities between innings. Each year the event grew, and by 2005, the activities spilled out of the gates and into the courtyard between the front offices and the ticket office. Inflatable bouncy houses, games, and obstacle courses occupied the narrow strip of sidewalk that ran between East 10th Street and the Erie Civic Center. Over the years, increased activities meant larger crowds and a healthier bottom line. For that reason, the spectacle grew and grew. The downside, though, was that we once again lacked the bodies necessary to supervise each of the activities. Even after soliciting local high schools for cheap (often volunteer) labor, we found that we were still shorthanded going into the birthday bash. This labor shortage was compounded by the fact that many companies and organizations that had mascots of some kind sent their costumes to the stadium, but never sent a body to fill it.

"I just don't know what else we can do," Rick explained a few days ahead of the event. "I have a village of bouncy houses and a prop room full of costumes, but there just aren't enough people to go around. Any ideas?"

At first, I had nothing. I thought of the previous year, trying to find one extra person willing to fill in for a twenty-minute press event with Channellock and the subsequent rejections offered by my oldest and closest friends. Only Renee had agreed to step in, but that hadn't gone particularly well either. But then again—Emmy was not Renee. Emmy was an NCAA student athlete. She lived an active lifestyle and did not fear sweat. On the contrary, she seemed to crave it, once explaining to me that "if you're not sweating, you're doing everything wrong." Not only that, Emmy was tough. Growing up in a family as one of eight kids, she had life experiences and a thick skin that was complemented by her unique perspective.

I looked at Rick then and said, simply, "I'll make a call."

It didn't take much convincing. Emmy was in. She even relayed my appeal to the rest of her family and came back with some good news.

"I got another one," she said.

At first, I thought she had made contact with one of her brothers. She had two that would be promising prospects. One was my age and finishing up his degree in computer science, and the other had just graduated from high school. Either one would have filled out a costume nicely.

"Oh, great! Tim? Devin?"

Emmy chuckled and said, "Lycia, actually."

Lycia was Emmy's thirteen-year-old sister and she was currently looking for some volunteer activities ahead of enrolling at the local college preparatory school. She wasn't whom I had in mind, but I was excited that Emmy was doing her best to help out, and I knew Rick would consider a volunteer from a local high school a bonus. So, as with every other time Emmy had ever bailed me out of a jam, I offered her my thanks and relayed the news to Rick.

***

The three of us arrived at the stadium together on gameday. Rick divvied out assignments and everyone took their stations. Originally, Lycia was listed with the mascots, but when her claustrophobia caused her to recoil from the head of a pink pig, she was immediately swapped out and placed in charge of one of the inflatable obstacle courses outside. Disappointment descended for one moment when one of my replacements was apparently not going to work out, but it lifted immediately when I caught a glimpse of that same pig, busting out a familiar dance move a short ten minutes later. I knew that pig by the way she moved—spunky and sexy, ebullient and equanimous. Inside that pink pig was Emmy.

I could have watched that pig move all day, but unfortunately C. Wolf made for a very popular birthday boy. So, I strut about as expected, greeting people at the gates, joking around with the kids, and throwing out the first pitch. I even had a go at some of the bouncy houses that were poised outside the gates. Whenever possible, I found Emmy and we watched the other mascots making fools of themselves on the field between innings. The most memorable of these was when Aslan, the lion from a local radio station, challenged the drunk duck from one of the local pubs to a bungee plunger toss. Attached at the waist by an elastic cord, they each had to scramble to fill their toilets with small plungers. No sooner had it begun when the drunk duck lost his head and ultimately the competition.

The next inning, the pink pig challenged me to a dance-off. U2's "Elevation" howled from the speakers and I started it off with a river dance—or something close to it. This was cheating to some degree, as it was the closest I could come to mimicking one of Emmy's hip hop routines, but as I was not as spry as she was, and had no idea what to do with my hands, the dance came off more Irish bouncy than East Coast thug.

Emmy countered my move with a shoulder shimmy. I answered that with a somersault, but came up short when Emmy shook her booty in a way that never failed to drive me (or the crowd for that matter) wild. I was transformed then, the voyeuristic big bad wolf, checking out the pig with the cutest damn tail, and suddenly I knew why he was always huffing and puffing in the storybooks. In the end, I'm pretty sure I lost the challenge. Then again, I was likely going to drive her home after the game, so I'm pretty sure I also ended up winning in the end.

Long after the mascot races and birthday cakes, when the game was over, I took Emmy and her sister back home. We showered, had dinner, and filled their siblings in on the goings on of the day.

Unlike Renee, Emmy had risen to the mascot challenge. Not only did she survive a day on the job, she had thrived in it. We were engaged in a year and married in two. I didn't know it then, but I would one day build a life with that perfect little pig. And though I know it took more than just this one day to fall in love, what Emmy gained from that experience was valuable insight. She learned about my job and about me. She saw me in the one venue doing the one thing that built my confidence above all others. Without C. Wolf, I'm not sure I'd have been a man who'd have held her eye. But even more, it gave her the perspective necessary to let me know when I was doing too much, and a means of letting me know when this chapter of my life, like all good things, would have to end.

False Stop

"I'm done."

Rick stared at me over his desk.

I had just finished my second season with the SeaWolves and that year had been particularly onerous. Between the countless injuries and chronic dehydration, I was popping Advil like they were Skittles in a vain attempt to quell body aches and migraines that just wouldn't go away. Since April of that year, I had logged over 400 hours in character, and with each one I could feel more damage mounting. In the final homestand of that year, even the minor stunts were taking a toll.

"What's that, C. Wolf?" Rick asked.

"I'm done," I said. "I just can't do this anymore."

"Okay," Rick said. "But the season's done. It's over. You did it."

"Yeah," I said simply. "But I'm just letting you know that I won't be back next season."

"Oh," Rick said, finally comprehending. "I gotcha. Well, I have to say that we'll miss you. Best mascot we've had, since I've been here anyway."

He said it as a genuine compliment, but by this time it was beginning to feel patronizing. After all, who couldn't just throw on that suit and do the idiotic things that I had been doing for the past two seasons? On those occasions when an injury or illness had kept me from working, there had always been another body, close at hand, ready to slip into C. Wolf and keep things moving.

Nobody ever seemed to notice, after all. It's not like anyone ever walked up to me after missing a game or two saying, "We missed you, C. Wolf. It's so good to have you back." All I ever heard was "Sign this" or "Get your ass over there now."

Rick stood up and reached across to me and shook my hand—a rare gesture to be sure.

"Really," he said. "Won't be the same here without you."

I wondered then if he were right.

***

Seven months later, I was finishing up my final spring semester at Edinboro University, and I had just received word that I was accepted into a graduate program at Slippery Rock University, just north of Pittsburgh. I was just beginning to consider my employment options for the summer when I fielded a call from none other than my old boss Rick.

After reading his name on the Caller ID, I waffled a bit. Should I answer it? What could he possibly want? For a moment, I considered the possibilities, then determining that the worst possible outcome would be a job offer that I would turn down, I decided to answer.

"Hello?"

"Hey, Dan." His voice was uncharacteristically cheerful. "It's Rick, from the SeaWolves."

"Hey, Rick. What's up?"

"Listen, I know you said you weren't going to be able to come back for us this year. I'm not calling to try and talk you into it, but I could really use some help."

"What kind of help?"

"We got this," he hesitated, "new guy. We've been trying him out for some of our appearances around town and—well—he sucks. Really. Really. He's just—he's terrible."

"Uh-huh. And how can I help with that?"

"Well, I was hoping that you might be able to come out and work with him a bit," Rick said. "We'd pay you your old rate for the time you put in. I just need you to—you know—teach him."

That was weird. For me the job was so innate that I struggled to imagine anyone "teaching" anyone anything. You slip into C. Wolf, you dance around like an idiot, and when you can hardly walk, you're done. It was that simple.

"Teach him? I asked. "Teach him what?"

"How to move, how to dance, how to interact with people. I mean, you are C. Wolf, for god's sake."

"I *was* C. Wolf," I corrected.

"Fair, but for the past two years you have been C. Wolf. The personalities, the instincts, you were inseparable. And now I'm over the barrel trying to figure out how to make this work without you and we have a lot of growing pains."

I didn't know how to respond. The guy before me was simply repurposed with the organization. He wasn't C. Wolf anymore, but he was still out there slinging popcorn and programs. Heck, the C. Wolf before that guy was still marching around selling beer out of a backpack in the reserved seating. If it they could curb his drinking in character, they had two ready-made replacements.

"What about Brian or Chad?"

"Brian can't do what you do," Rick said. "And Chad is—you know—Chad." He paused for a bit then before adding, "Plus, we already asked them."

***

The following Saturday, I wandered ghostlike through the ballpark gates. A little league tournament was underway and the concessions behind home plate were open, emitting the aroma of fresh-burst hot dogs on the grill. A few haunting cheers rose from the near-empty stands, a sound that was accented by the irregular ting of aluminum bats connecting with pitches.

Turning into the ticket office, familiar faces yattered into phones, handling the logistics of an imminent season opener just a few weeks off. None seemed to notice me passing by on my way down the hall to Rick's office. His door was closed, but the prop closet was open, so I stepped in and switched on the light. The freshly laundered new C. Wolf hung there beside the battered, locally made suit that I wore (and destroyed) during my first season, before the team deemed it worthwhile to pay for an upgrade. The vacant faces grinned down at me from the wire shelves. My heart pounded and hands shook as I stepped inside. It was almost like entering your childhood room after being away for years. It was just how I'd left it seven months ago. I was traveling back in time. I was coming home.

I sighed and reached out to touch one of the old uniforms. A shadow of a bloodstain encircled a handstitched seam where there was once a small tear, left behind by that teenager with a boxcutter. The sight caused my hand to rise, almost of its own accord, touching the approximate place on my body that bore the slight mark left by that same small blade. Memories rushed back—the good and the bad—and I almost forgot what had brought me back to that room.

"Hey, Dan."

Rick's greeting made me jump. In the doorway, Rick stood with a sandy-haired kid with a Justin Bieber bob whom I assumed would be my replacement.

"Dan, this is Corey. We're hoping that he'll be C. Wolf for us this year."

"Nice to meet you," I said, extending my hand, though Corey did not take it. Instead, he seemed to study it, warily, before nodding his greeting. His gaze never met my own.

Rick waved me off and mouthed the words "don't bother" to me, so I withdrew my hand and glanced around the prop room, awkwardly.

"So, Corey," Rick said. "Why don't you suit up? I'll have a chat with Dan here and we'll meet you outside when you're ready."

"Sure," Corey whispered.

We stepped outside the prop room, closed the door behind us, and I followed Rick outside onto the main concourse.

"I appreciate you coming out," Rick said, simply. "We've been searching for a new C. Wolf this whole off-season and things aren't going well. Corey here has been doing some of the promotionals for a while, but I'm afraid he's just not getting it."

"What's the main issue?"

"Well, he's got a few social hang-ups," Rick said. "He's a bit of a hypochondriac—or whatever it's called. Has an issue with germs and whatnot."

"He what?" I stared wide-eyed at Rick for a beat, wondering if I had heard him correctly.

"Yeah," he said. "It's a bit of a challenge. I have to launder the suit after every appearance."

"Every one?"

"Yeah. Can't really do that during homestands this summer. I tried to Febreze it once instead, but I guess he could tell. His mom threw a huge fit."

"Wait. His mom?"

"Oh, yeah," Rick cringed. "She's the hardest thing to deal with. But he is only sixteen and his mom is a little over-protective. Whenever I try to get something up on the calendar, I have to play twenty questions on the phone with her before I can get him scheduled. It's a real pain in the ass."

"And he's your *best* bet for this season?"

Rick shrugged.

When C. Wolf stepped out onto the concourse, he shuffled in our direction. C. Wolf turned to let Rick tuck his flap of neck fur into the padded muscle suit.

"All right, C. Wolf. Dan's going to coach you through a few things with the kids here for the tournament. Listen to him. He knows his stuff."

C. Wolf nodded and gave an awkward thumbs-up, but he didn't speak—odd given that (back then) C. Wolf was the only mascot in Minor League Baseball who talked. Rick and I followed behind as C. Wolf stumbled slowly in the direction of the open concession stand. He took short, tentative steps and appeared to be looking at the ground the entire way. As he rounded the corner by the concession stand, he was startled by a group of kids. He took a step back as they mobbed him, grabbing onto his legs, and hugging him around the waist. At first, C. Wolf looked like he wanted to run, then something switched on inside of him and he responded reluctantly. With a fat-fingered paw, he patted one of the children on the head, and when a parent wanted to take a picture, he stood stark still and rigid, as though he were trying to do his best impression of a statue.

"C. Wolf," I said, when the kids drifted back to their parents. "Why don't you try taking bigger steps. You know—just walk normally and keep your head up. Look around more."

C. Wolf nodded and then proceeded to take unnaturally large steps as though he were a child trying to step in his father's footprints in the snow. His nose pointed directly at the pavement, but then it swiveled back and forth. He wasn't just looking at his feet now, but instead he seemed to be scanning the entire ground directly in front of him as he moved along the concourse.

"Keep your head up," I called. "You want to look around and greet the people."

He did as I suggested, stopping first to look up at the empty bleachers. He offered it a half-hearted wave, then turned to acknowledge the few families seated along the third base stands. Then, without prompting, he turned back in our direction and walked back toward us, again with unusual, exaggerated steps. C.Wolf's nose swung back and forth like a pendulum as he went.

"Maybe you could teach him to do a somersault or something?" Rick suggested.

"A little early for that, don't you think?" I asked. "How about we get him to figure out the walking thing first?"

For the next hour, I coached Corey as best as I could, but we were clearly making little progress. He still couldn't move freely throughout the stadium without watching his feet, and he seemed to freeze whenever any personal interaction was required. Whenever I offered a suggestion, it seemed to make matters worse, triggering a bout of anxiety. Finally, options running out, Rick offered one last suggestion.

"Maybe you should try showing him?"

I shrugged. It seemed a reasonable suggestion, and it certainly couldn't have made things any worse.

We ducked into the prop room and Corey slipped free of the suit. Luckily, he didn't sweat much while he was inside, so the transition wasn't too uncomfortable. Five minutes later, I was back. I ran up and down the concourse and led a small group of parents in a cheer for the kids, who were wrapping up a game. I retrieved a hula hoop from the dugout. It was as if it were waiting for me, in the corner, right where I'd left it. I leapt onto the dugout, got the crowd clapping, and used it as a jump rope. Slowly I sped up, and the claps from the small crowd matched me, beat for beat.

My body remembered everything. Taut scars from the past years pulled at my skin. Muscles seemed to cramp prematurely, and I felt my neck once again straining under the weight of the head. But as this tiny group of parents and children flocked around me, none of that mattered. It was at that moment that I realized what Rick had meant when he said that I *was* C. Wolf.

When I finished my demonstration, I crawled out of the suit, sweaty but oddly satisfied. Rick grinned.

"So, Corey, care to give it another try?" Rick asked.

Corey glanced at me, then eyed the suit suspiciously. He shook his head.

"Not today. It needs cleaned."

"That's fine," Rick said simply. "Thanks for coming out. You can give your mom a call to come pick you up."

Corey nodded and left the office without another word, and Rick grinned knowingly. We stepped into his office, and he motioned for me to have a seat on the corner stool.

"So, what did you think?"

I stared at Rick, thinking about the past hour and a half, wondering how he could have selected Corey as my possible successor. A hypochondriac who seemed paralyzed by personal contact was not the obvious fit for a job that requires you to wear a suit that becomes so inundated with sweat during a game that it often does not have sufficient time to dry, festering away in the prop closet, before you have to put it on the next day. Then, I thought about how he had coaxed me back into the suit so easily.

"You never planned on hiring Corey for the season, did you?"

His grin grew a bit wider then. "Well, I was hoping it wouldn't come to that."

I realized only then that Rick had accomplished precisely what he had set out to do. He got me back inside. There I was too placated by the endorphins generated by being back to see the ulterior motives for what they were.

"So, Dan, what would it take for you to consider coming back?"

"I don't know if I can," I answered.

"You have another job lined up for the summer, then?"

I shook my head.

"So, theoretically, you're available and you'll need some sort of work, right?"

"I suppose, yeah."

"Well, what would it take? Give me a number. A spitball. Just throw something at me."

"I don't know," I said.

"Anything," Rob said. "Really. Just shout it out there."

I hesitated. "Maybe—double last year's rates?"

"That's it?" Rick asked.

I should have said triple, but once the number was out there, Rick stood and extended his hand without negotiation or argument. What I thought was a number completely out of the realm of possibility turned out to be precisely what he had been hoping for. I then thought of what that number meant. At double my rate from last year, I'd make more that summer than with any other job that I was considering. It'd more than cover my rent for that college apartment for the summer and even give me enough to squirrel away a modest savings ahead of my first year of grad school. Despite that, there were the physical factors to consider. Phantom pangs haunted my muscles at the thought of another season. Fifteen minutes in character that afternoon and it was as if every ache and pain I had experienced the previous year had reawakened. But it felt good to be out there again as well. It was nice to climb on the dugout and get even a small crowd chanting and clapping again. Pain or no, at least it'd keep me in shape for another year. Weighing all of the factors, I stood and accepted Rick's hand.

"Welcome back, C. Wolf!"

He said it so loud that there was a tiny hoot in the hallway. Rick rounded his desk and walked me out through the ticket office, and as I passed all the workers, so quiet and resolute at their desks when I'd arrived, they suddenly screamed with life and I was sent off to the applause of our beaming front office staff.

That day hadn't gone precisely how I'd expected, but I wasn't disappointed. It was good to feel wanted again, to feel appreciated for the work I had done and to have people excited for another year. As difficult as another season would be, it also meant that I had one more summer of minor celebrity status in my hometown. That meant one more summer at the ballpark, posing for photos, signing autographs—one more summer in a city full of people who'd be happy to see me wherever I went.

"You really think it will be worth it?" Emmy asked when I told her the *good* news.

"You don't?"

She thought about it for a moment then shook her head. "No. I don't have a good feeling about it. But it's your life. Do what you want."

Faltering Fourth

I arrived early at Iroquois High School on July 4, 2006. I had a day or two off since the previous homestand, but at that point, I was still a long way from feeling recovered. Recently my body had begun to rebel against my job. Apparently chronic dehydration and repeatedly raising your body temperature by wearing a fur suit at the height of summer has its complications. During the previous homestand, I had received intravenous fluids after almost every game. On one of these occasions, my blood sugar plummeted, and the paramedics included a very uncomfortable, shaky squeeze of glucose in the saline drip. I could feel the thick gel stretching the vascular walls all the way up my arm, leaving me with the sensation of a deep bruise that lingered for days.

On this particular day, I sat in my air-conditioned car chugging a Gatorade and waiting for a double dose of ibuprofen to kick in when a call rang through on my phone. It was Jessica, the marketing intern who, earlier in the season, had been tasked as my "handler." The title meant that, among her other duties with the team, she had the added responsibility of ensuring that I did not die on the job. I'm guessing this was largely due to the fact that my medical bills were starting to pile up and they were trying to keep the workman's comp claim within reason—but I can't really be sure.

I read her name on the caller ID, sighed, and flipped the phone open.

"Yeah?" I answered.

"We're here in the lineup." Jessica's voice seemed capable of spitting acid. "Where are you?"

"I just pulled in."

"Well then get your ass back here. They want us ready to go."

I glanced at the clock on the dashboard of my car.

"We've still got a half hour before this thing kicks off."

She sighed into the phone. Her breath crackled my ear. "Just get back here."

I killed the last of my Gatorade, snapped my phone shut, and opened the car door. The air hit me full in the face, like the heat blast from a sauna. The sun radiated off the blacktop, turning the entire parking lot into a giant solar oven, cooking me high and low. Not only that, but as the thick, stagnant air approached eighty degrees, the humidity hovered around ninety percent. As I retrieved the giant duffle bag from the trunk of my car, my head throbbed and my parched throat screamed in protest. A premonition followed, hanging over me like a black-winged curse. My whole body ached. This would not be a good day.

There were a few small trees along the side of the building, and I tried my best to hang in their shade as much as possible as I made my way to the back parking lot, pinned between school and stadium, where parade lineup was being organized. There, in the middle of the chaos, I saw the team van. Jessica sat in the driver's seat with two of the diamond girls—cute high school cheerleader types who were hired to help with on-field, gameday promotions.

"About time," Jessica spat from behind an oversized pair of bedazzled, faux designer sunglasses.

Working with her had become difficult, but it wasn't always. She had begun as a Diamond Girl when she was in high school. In those days, she was kind and understanding. However, when she was awarded one of the highly competitive internships with the SeaWolves, something changed. Most interns were timid as they learned the ropes during a single season, but having worked with the club for several years, Jessica had established a well of confidence. She knew what she was doing—or so she thought—and the front office management team gave her a bit more discretion than many of the others.

If you had met Jessica, you would instantly have known that appearances were important to her. While most interns wore baggy, unisex team polos, Jessica's team polos were tailored and form fitting. Her clothes had a way of hugging her curves and she always wore the right accessories with the right labels to make a statement. The overwhelming consensus was that Jessica "took care of herself." I only wish she would have shown half as much dedication to my wellbeing that season.

"You're not even ready?" Jessica said.

I rolled my eyes.

"Seriously?" she spat. "You're supposed to be a professional. I expected you to be ready."

"I will be," I said through gritted teeth.

"I don't mean ready when the cars start rolling," she said, waving around at the pickups, floats, and firetrucks that were idling in columns around us. "I mean ready ten minutes *before* we're rolling. Ready to run ahead and warm up the crowd before Caitlyn leans out the window and hits them with the T-shirt cannon."

"Fine, fine. Whatever."

I slid open the back door and crawled into the van. Without a word, I stripped down to my skivvies and slid into character. Pulling on the soft muscle suit, I realized how much my muscles still ached from the last game. Knots tightened in my calves and hamstrings, and my stomach cramped. Once dressed, I sat on the floor of that van and I did my best to loosen up, leaning this way and that, forcing the fibers of every muscle to stretch and contract in turn.

"You ready now?" Jessica asked, turning into the van and craning her neck to find me.

"Ready as I can be, I suppose."

She paused a moment, cocked her head, and shrugged. "Well?"

"Well what?"

"Get your ass out there!"

Better yet, I thought, *how about* you *put this thing on and get your ass out there!*

I couldn't bring myself to say that. For one reason, as my handler, she managed the schedule for all promotional events during that baseball season, and as such, she could seriously mess with the quality of my work life. Second of all, she had to sign off on my payroll and I suspected that she'd start shaving away hours that I'd worked just out of spite.

"Oh, you think you spent two hours in the suit today for this parade?" I imagined her asking. "Well, you did spend a lot of time in the van—so I think it was more like one."

So instead of arguing, I simply grunted, non-committally, strapped on the head, and rolled out of the air conditioning and into the sunlight.

On hot days, the first few minutes were deceptively easy. The inside of the head was still cool from the air conditioning, and having your face enveloped in shadow is not unlike carrying a portable shade with you. But that's at first. It didn't take long for the sun to penetrate the head's fiberglass shell, warming the air inside the mask. That, once combined with the heat produced by my own respiration, quickly raised the internal temperature in the suit well above that of the air outside.

During my first baseball season, friends often asked how hot it got inside that suit. It was a common question that I fielded incessantly, but I had no real idea of the number. So, during an afternoon game one weekend, I slid a thermometer inside the mask to see. This particular thermometer only had the ability to read up to 125° Fahrenheit (52° Celsius)—and this suit buried that needle. After that, I could only assume that it gets at least that hot in that suit. By the time the parade started moving, the inside of that suit was as hot as it had ever been.

The parade itself was a bit of a blur. I remember the people lining the driveway where the parking lot met the city, and the throngs of people gathered for several blocks. As instructed, I bolted ahead of the van, stopping to slap high-fives and take pictures with the families as we went. Whenever Jessica caught up with me, I darted back over, slapped the van's side (mainly because I knew this would annoy her). Then I crossed to the other side of the street to meet up with any kids that I might have missed. When the parade paused, the crowd chanted, and finally I sprinted along the street and threw myself into a customary front handspring. Every one of my muscles screamed when I did that. Each handspring I performed grew more and more difficult.

Five handsprings and four intersections into the parade, something started to feel very wrong. My cramped stomach was growing tighter and side stitches stabbed at my diaphragm. My field of vision wasn't so much blurred, but it seemed to be alive with static. Little pinpricks of light popped, swirled, and faded. Then I tried another handspring. My gloved paws hit the pavement, my elbows buckled, and I flopped, back flat against the street. It had been two years since I missed landing one of those. The muscles in my legs turned to jelly as I slowly drew myself up. The sound of cheers and applause slid in an out of focus, punctuated by the periodic thump of the T-shirt cannon flinging team memorabilia into the crowd. The static around me doubled. I staggered in the direction of the white blob that was the van pulling ahead of me on the street.

Even at the slow parade pace, it was difficult to catch up until the parade came to a stop. I fumbled for the door handle and pulled it open.

"The hell do you think you're doing?" Jessica asked, craning her neck in my direction.

I flopped onto the floor and unfastened C. Wolf's chinstrap. My chest heaved and I could feel my pulse beating inside my skull. In waves I felt my head grow heavy, then light, heavy, then light. Just as I lifted the mask enough to gulp a single breath of air-conditioned air, Jessica's temper ignited.

"No! Absolutely not."

"Breather," I huffed, trying to catch my breath.

"Are you kidding me? We're almost to the judges," she said.

"Can't," I panted. "Need a minute."

"Seriously," she said. "Get out there and earn your fucking paycheck!"

The van door was still open, but I pulled the head the rest of the way off despite that. I huffed and blinked in Jessica's general direction. I couldn't really see her. She was just a fuzzy silhouette. It was as though I had lost a contact lens inside the suit or something.

"Get your ass out there," she growled. "Do a fucking flip for the judges—and then you can have the rest of the afternoon for a fucking breather."

I glared at her.

"Don't look at me like that, C. Wolf. Just get out there."

The parade started to move again.

"NOW!"

I chewed on my lip, then took one last breath, as deeply as my lungs would allow. I pulled on the head and fell back out onto the street. Frustrated and exhausted, I tried my best to slam the door, which slid slowly on the track and closed with a weak *click*.

I could see the white chalked line on the street ahead of us that marked the beginning of the judge's zone. On the side of the road, there was a flatbed semi-trailer where three prominent members of the community were perched behind a folding table draped with red, white, and blue streamers. Then I heard a disembodied voice over a loudspeaker that announced each group as it approached the judges area.

"He howls, he growls, he bites, and he claws. He's fierce and furry, but there's no need to worry. He's everyone's favorite mascot—C. Wolf!"

The crowd cheered as the van rolled into the line. The *thunk, thunk* of the T-shirt cannon sounded on one side of me. Some shirts dropped onto people along the street, while I heard other shirts snagged in the trees as gravity took them.

The van pulled away from me so I kicked into a run—and I immediately regretted it. Pain erupted in my every extremity. My body protested each step I took, until I threw myself into a handspring. I landed—barely. My knees buckled at the far edge of the judges box, and suddenly it was as though I were underwater, moving in slow motion. The air thickened, bending the light until the street signs, the storefronts, the lampposts, and people were twisted like reflections in a funhouse mirror. They were melting away. They weren't real— they couldn't be. I was falling then, all sound muffled, the last of my vision going. Something tore at me then and the touch was agony.

"Oh my God, C. Wolf? Are you okay?" It was a familiar voice, but it wasn't Jessica. Maybe it was Caitlyn. Maybe one of the others. "We have to get him out of this," the voice came again. "I think he's crying."

***

I came to, burning with cold. There was an IV tugging at the back of my hand and a saline drip on a rod above my head. I felt something cold running through my veins, up my arm to my shoulder. I could feel a chill seeping through my head. At my feet C. Wolf's wide eye and manic smile stared into my soul and I shivered violently.

"It's all right." A man in shorts and a T-shirt was grinning at me. He wore an orange baseball cap and had a Super Mario Brother's mustache. "You gave those girls a bit of a fright back there."

I tried to raise my arm, realizing only then that I had been strapped to a gurney and then I registered the sound—of a siren. An ambulance. I gave my head a shake, and my brain rattled inside of my skull. The strange man tapped on the door to the front of the ambulance and the driver killed the siren.

"What happened?"

"Heat and dehydration, I'd wager. Your blood pressure was pretty low, and when I tried to get the IV in at first, your veins were laying flat as a pancake. It was a bear to get that going for you." He nodded to the bag of saline swaying overhead. "Feeling better?"

"I think," I said.

"Yeah, I thought that'd help," the man grinned. "Sometimes when there's a really hot day, I give myself one of those. A little saline can make you feel like a new man."

An involuntary shiver stole my body again and I felt something hard and cold packed around my crotch and up my armpits. The man pulled back the sheet that was draped over me and I saw that I was naked—or very nearly anyway. A pair of boxers is all that separated me from the sheet. For a moment I thought of a similar sheet that I'd seen before. It had been draped over a body at the scene of an accident I saw once when I was younger. Suddenly I was very creeped out.

"Cold?" the man asked. He leaned forward and plucked the bags of ice out from under my armpits. Then, unabashedly, he reached down the front of my boxers and pulled out a bag that he had tucked down under while I was out. Then he pulled the sheet back over me.

"What the hell?" I said.

"Hey, best way to bring down your core temp. You were up around 104 when we got you out of that suit. Once you get up to 106 things start shutting down. Can go bad quick from there."

I shook my head, then glanced back toward C. Wolf. The head smiled blankly at me. Then I noticed that most of him was missing.

"Where's the rest of him?"

"Oh, the girls have him."

I nodded, then wondered aloud. "Why didn't they grab the head?"

"Oh, that," the man shook his head. "That one girl back there is a piece of work."

He glanced at the saline drip and gave a little chuckle.

"She didn't want us taking the head off," he finally said, then raised the pitch of his voice into a mocking female tone. "You can't take the head off. You'll ruin it for the kids if they see that. Do that and you'll ruin the magic."

Again, my eyes rolled inside my skull. "That'd be Jessica."

"Yeah, well someone should have a talk with her," the man said. "I explained that we had to get you clear of the suit. You could have died in there. So, I took out a pair of scissors and was going to cut you out and she screamed at me." The pitch of his voice raised again and I could practically hear Jessica's voice saying, verbatim, "No! Do you have any idea how much that suit costs? You cut that and my boss will have *my* head!" His voice dropped again and his chuckle amplified into a full-fledged laugh. "Then—"

He buried his face into the palm of his blue-gloved hand and his shoulders heaved as the memory rose to the forefront of his mind.

"Then—then," he continued, fighting the laughter, "she had the other two strip you from the neck down. They undid the zipper and just peeled that fur off you in one giant piece! But— they left that head."

159

Suddenly I understood why he found this so funny. Imagine a giant, incapacitated wolf lying in the middle of the street, concerned families watching, unable to shield the eyes of the innocent as two teenage girls removed his skin, like a hunter peeling the pelt from a fresh kill. I envisioned then the faces in the crowd, the blushing of mothers, embarrassed by a flash of nudity, the tear-stained cheeks of children, screaming at the sight of C. Wolf's *murder*. Then—as a bonus—I saw this man in his orange ballcap packing the carcass with ice—trying his best to preserve it for the freezer. I felt myself snigger at the thought of my freakishly thin torso still topped with that massive head. How much would it have looked like a long-haired dog that had been shaved from the neck down, the juxtaposition of that fuzzy head with its now-bare body?

"Anyway," the man continued, "she told us to keep that head on you until we got you out of sight."

My chuckle fell away then as the implications of his words washed over me. In my own mind I now imagined me in distress, laying on the street for an eternity as Jessica argued with the EMTs over mascot etiquette while I could have been dying there at her feet.

"Wait." I glanced back to C. Wolf's head. "You mean you listened to her?"

We hit a bump as we pulled into the ambulance entrance of Hamot Medical Center, and the dismembered head appeared to nod back at me.

"Yeah," the man's smile faded and he appeared more than a little embarrassed. "Sorry. Probably wasn't the best call on our part."

Dumbfounded, I wanted to tell him off then, but the doors of the ambulance opened and the man clicked something under the gurney. I was wheeled out, but before I crossed the threshold of the building, I caught a glimpse of my transport. And in an instant my frustration with the man with the Mario mustache ebbed away at the sight of the words "Volunteer Fire Department."

That explains it, I thought. *I guess you get what you pay for.*

***

The first face that greeted me in the ER was not the one I expected. Jessica poked her head around the glass partition and peered between a gap in the curtain.

"Hey," she said, her voice more diminutive than she had been in the van. She looked as though she might have been crying too. "Brought you your things."

She stepped in and placed my clothes on the chair in the corner of the room, but didn't look at me directly.

"Thanks," I said.

"Oh, I used your phone to call Emmy," she said. "I thought you might want her here. Anyway, she's on her way."

For a while, she stood there, silent, and I felt the urge to tell her off.

It's all your fault, you know, I thought, biting my lip. *I told you I needed a break. I told you something was wrong. And why the hell were you arguing with those EMTs?*

I wanted to say all this and more, but her wet eyes glistened. Her worried expression had softened the stony features of her face, and she looked pitiful. My desire to tell her off diminished, bit by bit, until it was gone completely. She just stood there, waiting until Emmy arrived. The two of them exchanged pleasantries, then Jess headed back to the office, I assumed to file an incident report with Rick.

When I was finally discharged, the official diagnosis was acute dehydration and heat exhaustion, though the resident who had overseen my treatment that afternoon said that, based on his experience, I had been well on my way to heatstroke and that's when things would have gotten a lot worse.

When Emmy and I left the hospital, we went straight to the front office. Rick had called and said that I needed to sign some paperwork when I got the chance, and I figured now was as good a time as any. When I stepped into his office, Rick let out an audible sigh and a big smile. He leaned back in his chair and laced his fingers behind his head.

"Welcome back," he said simply. "You had us all really worried there for a bit."

I handed him the papers the ER had given me, including a note that I was to take it easy for the next few days. He considered these papers and nodded.

"Makes sense," he said. Then he called Jessica in and handed her the papers with instructions to make copies and file them. "So, what happened anyway? Jess said you just kind of went down at the end of the parade."

"That's not exactly—"

I paused. For an instant, I thought about telling him everything—how she ordered me out of the van when I tried to take a breather, not to mention what the EMT with the Mario mustache had told me about the argument that ensued regarding the etiquette of removing a mascot's head in public. But then I remembered Jess's face in the ER. She looked worried, scared, and more than a little guilty and my desire for vengeance seemed to wane then. I was already exhausted and just wanted to go home with Emmy and lay down on the couch. So, I just shrugged.

"I guess I don't really know," I said finally. "Maybe we'll just have to chalk it up to occupational hazard?"

"Yeah, you've had a knack for finding those lately." He fingered his computer monitor and grinned uncomfortably.

When I left the front office, I climbed into the passenger seat of the car where Emmy was waiting. She reached over to my hand and stroked the back of the bandage where the IV had been. When my eyes found hers, she raised an eyebrow and asked a question she had posed to me so many times.

"Well?" she began. "Was this worth it?"

Meeting Bobby Lee

The Saturday before Christmas in 2005, I prowled the halls of the local VA hospital as C. Wolf, bearing bags of salt-free pretzels for veterans who were expected to remain admitted through the remainder of the holiday season. Some were relatively young, about my age at the time, seeking treatment for ailments that lingered after their tours in Iraq and Afghanistan were concluded. Yet others were older, having fought in Vietnam, Korea, and World War II.

One of the administrators led me up and down the corridors with the list of room numbers on her clipboard. Most of the time, the visits were relatively short. I popped in, shook some hands, and lay a bag of pretzels on the bedside trays before continuing on to the next soldier or sailor on the list. Few had visitors, and some simply napped through the entirety of my visit. The whole of the afternoon had been relatively unremarkable; that is until I found myself outside the last door that was on our list.

"I just want to give you a little heads up," said one of the hospital administrators. She was a well-dressed, middle-aged woman with bottle-blonde hair. "He's been here a while and probably will be until—you know. He's a little angry about that. Sometimes he takes it out on people."

I nodded, doing my best to process the information, but I wasn't sure then why it was so important. None of the other patients warranted this sort of sidebar. I wondered why this stop was any different.

She pushed open the door and stepped inside. I hung back behind the curtain, just out of view.

"Oh, for Christ's sake," a hoarse baritone rattled behind the curtain. "What are yinz bothering me with now? More blood? Bunch of goddamned leaches."

"No, Mr. Lee," the administrator said in a measured professional tone. "I'm just here because you've got a visitor."

"So excited to get rid of me you had to lead death to me, personally?"

The administrator shook her head and she motioned to me. I straightened up and, while holding a bag of pretzels outstretched in both hands, I walked into the sterile, blue-walled room. There were tubes and machines in there, though none, except the saline drip, seemed to be hooked up. I turned to face a steely-eyed man who glowered at me uncertainly. His face was weathered and unshaven, and with a half-grunt, half-cough, the old man attempted to clear his throat.

"And what is this all about?" the old man said, fumbling for one of the buttons on his hospital bed. The mechanism whirred and his head slowly began to rise.

"It's C. Wolf," the administrator introduced me. "He's here to pay you a little visit.

The old man nodded skeptically.

"Oh. All right," he said, motioning to the chair at his bedside. "So, are you gonna sit down, or what?"

I hesitated and offered a glance toward the administrator. She blinked, seemingly surprised by the invitation, then offered me a half shrug.

I crossed the room, and as I did so, Mr. Lee extended a hand in greeting. I shook it and handed him the bag of salt-free pretzels. He laid it on the tray table that extended over his lap with his untouched lunch. I settled into the seat beside him. He studied me suspiciously for a moment, then turned back toward the administrator.

"Isn't there someone else around here for yinz to torture or something?"

The administrator smiled without humor.

"Well?" Mr. Lee growled. "Go on. Get out of here and let me talk to the wolf."

"I'll be back in a while to check on you then," the administrator said, and after I offered her the thumbs-up, she stepped outside the door."

I turned back to face Mr. Lee, who eyed me suspiciously. It was as if he were trying to decide if I were friend or foe.

"So, Mr. Lee," I began in C. Wolf's usual growl.

"Name's Bobby," he said. "You know. Like that old Confederate general, Bobby Lee. But he died before my time. We were related, you know. Don't remember exactly how just now. Shit they give us here, messes with your mind."

"Oh, right. Bobby then. So what service were you with?"

"Army," he said, "but I spent twenty years working as a Back Country Ranger after that."

"Back Country Ranger?"

"Yeah," he said simply. "In the wilderness areas out west—up in the Rockies mostly."

"What was that like?"

His expression softened. "Amazing. Best job ever."

Something flashed in his eyes and it seemed to cut through his cold countenance. Through it I gained the glimpse of my own grandfather, the old Army Air Corps soldier who died before I had a chance to really know him. Although I had just met Bobby Lee, there was something about him that piqued my curiosity. Everyone has a story, after all. All you need is someone to listen.

"What sort of things did you do out there?"

"Patrolled a lot of the trails to make sure people followed the rules. Had to carry in whatever supplies you need and carry everything out with you when you left. Leave only footprints—that's the code."

"I think I've heard something about that from my dad," I said. "When he's talking about backpacking."

"Yeah? You like camping? Backpacking?"

I shrugged. "We did a lot of camping, as a kid. My dad liked backpacking, but I never tried it."

"Ah, you should, especially out west. Does a lot of good. When I got out of the Army, people were hard for me, but out there, I worked the trails, usually with horses or mules. They were one of my favorite bits. People they'll bite for nothing at all. But horses—they only bite if there's a reason. There's always a reason."

I sat there for over an hour, never removing one bit of C. Wolf. I was simply a giant wolf listening to stories of the wilderness and learning how that mission helped one man to recover from the other missions in Korea—a war that made little sense to the man who had fought twice for the city of Seoul. He tensed up, talking more to himself than to me about combat. He explained how useless the doctors were, telling him to "just act normal and you'll feel normal." But when he spoke of the wilderness, something in him came alive again, and he smiled, sharing stories of how he repurposed his military experience to hunt down poachers who dared to defile what he claimed was "God's last true cathedral."

When the administrator came back, I stood and shook the hand of Bobby Lee.

"You come back and see me again soon," he said, and he gripped my hand with a renewed strength that I did not expect from a man of his age and condition.

I assured him I would, and I waved back as I followed the administrator into the hall. She beamed, eyes wide, as she led me back to her office, where my duffle bag was stowed.

"I don't get it," she said. "That man has been miserable to everyone since he got here. But you plop a guy in a wolf suit next to him and it's like he's just catching up with an old friend."

I think it was really people that made him lash out like that. By that I don't mean the well-intentioned doctors and nurses who provided care for soldiers and sailors that Christmas. I think it was most likely the generals who had thrown him into battle all those years ago. Perhaps it was the bootstrap politicians, the generation of post-war psychologists who had urged Mr. Lee to just not think about those things—to ignore them until they went away. Or maybe it was just the fact that the chair for visitors next to his bed had simply remained vacant too long. Maybe when you're let down by people so often in life, there are things that you can say to a giant wolf that others just wouldn't understand.

After the new year, I returned to the VA to honor my word to Mr. Lee, but when I arrived, his bed was filled by another. I asked about him at the nurses' station, by name and room number.

"Oh, Mr. Robert Lee?" a nurse said.

She consulted the computer and took a long pause. Then she clucked her tongue and shook her head.

"I'm afraid that he's no longer with us," she said.

The answer struck me as a vague, curious choice of words. At the time I couldn't tell whether that meant that old Bobby Lee had passed away or whether he had simply gone home, or found his way to a hospice or other long-care facility. The nurse refused to provide any further clarification and privacy laws being what they were, I suppose I understood that.

Whatever happened to Bobby Lee after I left, I was glad to have had the chance to meet him, if only to give him an opportunity to remember his time in the backcountry. In some way, as he told me his stories, it was like his mind was freed from that bed. In that retelling, he didn't appear to be a seriously ill patient, nor was I just a second-rate mascot from the local Minor League Baseball team. It was like he was a ranger again, patrolling the trails, and I was a lone wolf that he met along the way. At the VA that Christmas, we traveled that waning wilderness together, reminding each other that—at least in that moment—we both were very much alive.

Autographs

It is really fascinating to think about the things we human beings covet. We covet shiny, tangible things like silver, gold, and diamonds. We covet mundane things, like clothes, photo albums, and old, busted-up cars. We covet new things and old things, big things and small things. We covet things for sentimental reasons, for perceived value, but often we seem to covet things because the people around us do.

In the world of professional sports—even in the minor leagues—memorabilia are highly prized. Whether it comes in the form of jerseys, balls, bats, bobbleheads—if it's officially licensed, people will pay a premium for it. If you want to further increase the amount people are willing to pay for something, the easiest way is to find someone on the team's payroll willing to autograph it. It doesn't really matter who it is (most of the time you can't read the names anyway). All that matters is that the scribbler in question adds some sort of perceived value.

The first time I observed the correlation between perceived value and autographs was not in a ballpark or hockey arena, but on a high school marching band trip to Orlando, Florida. A few of my friends and I had just visited the gift shop at Planet Hollywood where I purchased a new pair of sunglasses and shirt. As we settled in at the table for dinner, one of my friends made an observation.

"You look just like a young Tom Cruise," he said.

"Whatever," I answered, though I had heard others make this comparison before. Just for fun, I slipped on my shades, cocked my head, and gave him a little *Risky Business* smile.

"Dude, you totally do," he insisted. Then a thought came to him. "I just had a crazy idea."

That night we hatched a plan and decided to try it out when we returned to Downtown Disney for lunch. I hovered between shops, wearing my new slick shades and new shirt while my buddy waited around the corner. When a group of tourists approached, he ran up to me—wearing my slick shades and brand-new shirt—and asked me to take a picture with him and to sign his souvenir bag. I did both, gladly, then turned to see a queue forming behind him. For fifteen minutes, I signed autographs and took pictures with people, many visiting from other countries, and none knew who I was, let alone who I was supposed to be. All they knew was that someone else had asked for my autograph and a picture, and they now wanted one too.

I was reminded of that trip years later, after a game at Jerry Uht Park. As I exited the ticket office on my way to the showers after a game, I was stopped by Jackie, the twelve-year-old daughter of one of our season ticket holders, whom I nicknamed "Sticky Hands" on account of her always eating cotton candy whenever I saw her at a game. For the record, she never seemed to mind the nickname. I had met her outside the suit several times and I was friendly with her father, who was a professor at the same college I was attending. When I saw her and her dad waiting by the gates, I noticed that she was brandishing a new souvenir bat, which I think must have been the giveaway for that game.

"Oh—I didn't catch you today, but could you sign my bat for me?" she asked.

"Sure," I said, not thinking anything of it.

She handed me the bat and the Sharpie that she always carried and I scribbled "C. Wolf #00" on the end of the bat, chatting with her a bit about her dad and their plans for the rest of the summer. As I handed the bat back to her, I noticed a cluster of parents watching me, forming into a makeshift line with their kids, reaching for whatever they had on them at the time. I stood there for an extra half hour or so, scribbling "C. Wolf" on everything that was presented, and as I did so, I was immediately reminded of that trip to Orlando in high school. I had become accustomed to signing things while in the suit— but in a torn pair of soccer shorts and a sweaty SeaWolves T-shirt, it felt a bit surreal. I looked more like a vagrant than any sort of celebrity. Nobody knew who I was before I signed, but just because one twelve-year-old girl asked me to sign something, people waited en masse for me to sign things, despite the fact that I was drenched with sweat and smelled of hot garbage.

As I mentioned before, autographs carry a perceived value, but what I learned on the job is that this perception is entirely wrong. True, an autograph from a specific player at the right time in history can add value to even the most mundane object. However, most autographs run the risk of actually devaluing the item that is being signed. To illustrate that point, consider the time when C. Wolf met Justin Verlander.

Justin Verlander passed through Erie, staying for just two weeks on his way to the majors. One day, before pitching, he was stationed at the autograph table behind the third base grandstands. I had never seen such pomp for a minor league player. He was a top prospect for the Detroit Tigers, and the entire organization knew that he would only be in Erie for a few weeks. The SeaWolves organization did everything that they could to capitalize on his time there.

Just as he finished signing before the game, Rick called me over and introduced me (as C. Wolf) to a man who would become one of the most dominant pitchers for the next decade. The introduction wasn't much, just a few words and a handshake while I was in costume. I have to admit, after the big deal everyone had made, even I was kind of excited to meet the guy. But what was even more interesting came later that day, when it was my turn to occupy the autograph table during the eighth inning.

When the announcement came across the PA system, the standing-room crowd began filtering past on their way to the stadium gates, many stopping to have me sign their memorabilia. Most of it had already been signed by Justin. So, I picked a spot near his autograph and scribbled my own signature right next to it. As I did so, I imagined the grandchildren of one of these fans on a future version of *Antiques Road Show*, seeking some valuation on SeaWolves memorabilia far into the future.

"What a treat this is," the imaginary expert said. "Do you have any idea what you have here?"

"No—none," the fan responded, repressing the urge to grin. "My grandfather was a huge baseball fan and he left this for me when he passed."

"What you have here is an early autograph from Hall of Famer pitcher Justin Verlander," the expert in my head said. "Now this ball is from the Eastern League, so I can assume that this is from his short stint—of about four weeks—that he spent in Erie, Pennsylvania, back in 2005."

The fan, in my head, oohed and ahhed then, as the expert pointed out what made this autograph truly unique.

"Now, Verlander is a pretty common signature, but then you have this other name," he said pointing at my autograph. "This is largely a mystery to us. Who was this mystery player? Nobody knows, but every now and again when we find an early Verlander autograph, this name is also there. That is what makes this piece particularly rare—and all the more special."

I fought the fantasy and continued signing, finishing each with a bit more of a flourish, as the future appraisal played over and over in my head. Perhaps it was my subconscious trying to convince me that I was doing the fans a favor. How could I possibly be devaluing these pieces of memorabilia by scribbling my name next to his? Plus, they were asking for it. I was simply obliging them, bestowing upon them a gift by realizing that perceived value for each of them. But deep down I knew the truth. There was no mystery; just a twenty-one-year-old college student wearing a wolf's head, taking pleasure in halving the true value of these personal treasures—nothing more.

A Kid Named Jack

(For Jack Armbruster)

In 2013, I was settling in at my computer, bracing for another interminable weekend of grading for my writing classes at the University of Wisconsin—Stout. I filled my mug from the cozy-clad teapot on the table beside me, and sipped tentatively from it as I did my best to procrastinate, occupying myself with anything that could keep me from the course shells in the Desire 2 Learn course management system. First, I sifted through my emails, beginning with those from work, then moved methodically through each of my subsequent personal accounts. I conducted a series of internet searches, looking for nothing in particular, but ultimately learning that I could own all eleven seasons of the television show $M*A*S*H$ for only $90 on Amazon—a bargain I just couldn't pass up. So, I placed an order.

When I exhausted all other options, I turned my attention to the thing that I hated almost as much as grading, my old Facebook profile. It arguably served no purpose at this time in my life, other than existing for those common occasions when someone asked "Are you on Facebook?" so that I could say "yes" without alienating myself further from the social conventions of modern society. There I found the usual, a handful of friend requests from people who hated me in high school, a few Facebook messages, and the odd phishing scam or two. But as I clicked through the notifications and perused my messages, one stood out to me. It was from someone whom I once knew very well, someone whom I occasionally found myself wondering about from time to time.

"Hey, Wolfy!" the message read, and I could hear it punctuated by a croaky, high-pitched growl of an eight-year-old boy. "I hope you remember me. I saw you on here and thought I'd say hi. Write me back when you get a chance."

For a while, I read and re-read the message, sipping from my oversized mug of tea, and found myself remembering things that I had long forgotten.

***

Back in 2006, I sidled out through the ticket office door and onto the main concourse behind the third base reserved seats. I passed by the concession stand toward a folding table where one of the pitchers who was not scheduled to throw sat, signing pregame autographs for the fans. There were games to keep the kids busy—a fast-pitch radar gun and a beanbag toss—each manned by a volunteer from one of the local high schools. Ultimately, I found my way to the picnic garden, where Jack Armbruster was waiting alongside a table with balloons and streamers. His mom and dad were there, as was his older sister, Ellen. When he saw me approach, Jack's face lit up.

"C. Wolf!" he called, grinning through his braces.

"Hey, I heard someone was having a birthday party today," I said.

"Yeah, it's my party!" Jack beamed.

"Oh yeah? How old are you then? Twenty? Twenty-one?"

"Eight," Jack answered.

"Twenty-eight? You're looking pretty good for your age, eh?"

"No, not twenty-eight?"

"Oh? Thirty-eight?"

"NO! I'm eight. Eight."

"Eight, eight? Eighty-eight?"

This was one of my favorite gags with the birthday kids. Jack's mom laughed, as he leaned forward, squinting at me, eyebrows low and fighting a smile. He growled.

"I'm just eight, Wolfy."

"Oh," I said, playing it dumb. "I don't suppose eight-year-old kids like cake, do they?"

"Yes!" he grinned.

I motioned to the intern who was carrying a box that held a sheet cake behind me. She slid it onto the table and I produced the small, cube-shaped box that had been tucked neatly in the palm of my hand. I extended it to him and Jack took it from me.

"Happy birthday, Jack!" I said.

"Thanks, Wolfy!"

His mom helped him to open the box and inside was a baseball, autographed by the entire team. He studied the ball. One of the things I remember most about Jack is that he never stopped smiling, and it was a contagious condition.

"Well," I said, after a few minutes. "What about my payment?"

He glared skeptically up at me then.

"I think," I said, scratching my chin before extending a paw, "I'm running a birthday special today. So, I'll just take four."

Jack grinned, then he wound up, almost like a pitcher on the mound, twisting in his chair and connecting with the hardest high-five he could muster. On contact, my paw flung back and I spun around on my way to the ground, landing harder than I had intended on the pavement, padded only slightly by my tail. Chortling, he and his sister each grabbed a paw and helped me back to my feet and I posed for their annual birthday picture, back for another season at Jerry Uht Park.

Throughout the day, I entertained the crowd the best that I could, taking care to stop by to see Jack as often as possible. I'd sit in an empty seat beside him and often teased him or his sister. That game, like most of those that Jack attended through the years, moved fast, and before I knew it, I watched a long fly ball hit toward center field. The players shifted and I lost sight of the ball in the clouds. That is, until Curtis Granderson settled under it and snagged the ball cleanly in the pocket of his mitt.

"It's time!" Jack cried over the cheering crowd in the box seats behind home plate.

I glanced to the scoreboard. It was the sixth inning and—as usual—I had lost track of time. In two outs, I was due behind the outfield wall and, in all honesty, I should have been there already.

"Shit," I hissed under my breath. It was almost time for the kid stampede and I had to be there.

Since I started working in baseball, I wondered why this promotional even existed. The umpires hated it, it was nothing but a headache for the staff, and then there were the liability issues. There was no rational reason that this event had to happen. Yet, it was scheduled for virtually every game.

"Come on. This way, Wolfy," Jack called again. "Follow me!"

I turned back to where he was sitting. He was there no longer. With no peripheral vision, I craned my neck for any sign of where he'd gone. Then I glimpsed his mother and sister near the stadium gates and knew immediately where he was.

I sprinted outside, emerging onto the sidewalk just in time to see him in his souped-up wheelchair, zipping around the corner.

"Come on, Wolfy! You'll never beat me," Jack chided.

When I finally caught up with him, he was already parting the mob of children and parents who had gathered behind the center field wall. Once in position, he spun round in his chair to see where I was. One of the Diamond Girls followed Jack's line of sight and found me.

"Hurry up, C. Wolf!" she shouted at the top of her lungs. "Last out!"

Winded, I rushed along the path that Jack had cleared before the bodies could close in again, and I leaned against the gate to catch my breath.

"Took you long enough," Jack smirked. "You gettin' tired?"

"Nah," I groaned. "Just resting up. Got more than enough in the tank to smoke you."

"You wish."

His wheelchair whirred as he spun back to watch the last bit of action through the gap in the center of the gates. The two quick outs from earlier in that inning were followed by a series of hits and walks that seemed to take forever. The muscles in my legs began to cramp as we waited for the gates to open. The air grew thick as the kids en masse pressed in behind us.

"Back it up," the Diamond Girls yelled, as two of them unrolled a length of rope. "Behind the line. Go on, go on. Back. Back. BACK!"

The Diamond Girls and interns did their best to give us some space, but there was only so much that they could do with an old piece of clothesline. Order continued to devolve. The collective fuse of the anxious children ignited. The mob smoldered and seethed behind us. Chaos was imminent.

"That's strike three," a voice buzzed over the radio. "Let 'em loose."

"This is it!" Jack shouted.

At his words, the crowd ripped the rope from the hands of the Diamond Girls and everyone surged forward. Two of the interns removed the chain from the gate and a school bell rang out over the PA system followed by the theme song from *Saved by the Bell*. The crowd behind us pushed forward, before the outfield wall opened, pinning Jack and me and the interns against the chain link. I pushed back against the bodies, until there was just enough daylight for Jack to drive his wheelchair out onto the field. He bolted and I followed immediately behind, with what seemed every child in the tri-state area on our heels. The force of the massive crowd pushing on the gates slammed them open, and the interns did their best to sidestep the action without getting trampled.

My heart pounded and I struggled to force air into my burning lungs through the sweltering mask, a problem that seemed not to trouble Jack. He screamed and roared, as his chair tore across the turf and I dug into the ground with the toes of my oversized, clownish shoes, charging behind him. As I pulled even, Jack jabbed at his controls, cutting me off, first to the right, then to the left. The mob behind ran to the side, making a beeline for the open gate to the right field stands. But Jack and I took the longer way around, hugging close to the warning track, heading for the wheelchair ramp that was installed beside the visiting team's bullpen. We were almost across the field. Now was the time to make my move. I threw my body forward, racing even with Jack. Leaning forward in his chair, he glanced my way and extended a hand. I took it and we finished, crossing the warning track together, his curled fingers clamped tight in my paw.

That was the Kid Stampede. While Jack and I climbed the wheelchair ramp behind the visitor's bullpen, a few others following behind us, I surveyed the crowd still on the field. As usual, the kids were bottlenecked at the gates that led back into the stands, and many were now standing in a horde that trailed into the outfield, delaying play. The umpires shook their heads and checked their watches as they scanned the gathering mob. Yes, it was a headache for many of the adults, but it was the highlight of the game for the children, who got to spend a few minutes on the field, gazing up at the screaming crowd. Most, I'm certain, imagined themselves as players, taking the field of a sold-out stadium. For Jack, I'm sure, it was no different. Face alight, he beamed, just a kid in a sea of other kids, finding joy in a few precious moments in the outfield. Nothing that happened at any game made him happier.

At the time, Jack had been the Pennsylvania goodwill ambassador for the Muscular Dystrophy Association. He was once the youngest regional ambassador in the history of the MDA, offered the honor at the ripe old age of three, and he was probably one of the cutest and most uplifting kids I had ever known.

I shook off the memories and smiled, glancing at the date stamp on the Facebook message. He had sent it to me earlier that week—September 18—and I drafted a quick response to him and sent it on Saturday, September 21.

"Hey, Jack!" I began. "Of course, I remember you. It's great to hear from you. How've you been?"

I went on a bit more than that, I'm sure, probably mentioning where I had moved at the time, the new job teaching in Wisconsin, and shared the news that I had gotten myself married. Message sent, I finally turned my attention to my courses, where it really should have been all along, and downloaded a batch of essays and began to read.

I checked Facebook daily for a while, anticipating some kind of a response from Jack. He had been on my mind a lot since I read his message and I was genuinely looking forward to hearing how his life was turning out. Days slipped into weeks, weeks into a month. Soon it was November.

I didn't expect a response from him to take that long. Curious, I turned back to our common friends' Facebook profiles and learned the sad news. Jack, just sixteen years old, had passed away on September 20, just one day before I had read his message.

Learning of his death was a shock. Despite his physical challenges, Jack was always vibrant. Life radiated out of him. He didn't just touch the lives of everyone he came into contact with—he improved them in very tangible ways. Thinking back, it is impossible to express what it meant to have the privilege of knowing Jack.

As my career as C. Wolf wound down, I was always exhausted and in a fair bit of pain, but when Jack was around, he had a way of making you forget whatever was ailing you. I'm sure some of it was perspective; after all, it's hard to complain about cramping muscles and aching joints when you're hanging with a wheelchair-bound eight-year-old. But more than that, Jack lived by example. He was never closed off to a new experience and he accepted people as they came, faults and all.

It Was the Best of Jobs; It Was the Worst of Jobs...

The 2006 baseball season was nearing its end, and I was exhausted.

There was a new start on the horizon. I had just been accepted into a graduate program at Slippery Rock University, Emmy and I had just signed the lease on our first apartment together, and the word "engagement" had been floating phantomlike in the air between us. Yes, life was moving on, and for the first time, I knew definitively that I would not be taking these next steps alone. With all this happening, it made sense that this would be my last season in Minor League Baseball. Was it a logical decision? Yes. Easy? No.

Although each year I had discovered new and exciting ways to injure myself, that last season felt different. Where previous seasons had left me with minor strains, sprains, and separated shoulders, 2006—the climax of my career—had landed me in the ER, packed with ice, dehydrated, and on the verge of heatstroke. Post-game IVs and Gatorade spiked with glucose were becoming quite routine. In previous seasons, I probably would have sucked it up, ignored the signals that my body had been sending me, and kept on going despite it all. But as fortune would have it, I wasn't alone. Emmy watched me, and with each game she appeared more distressed by it all.

In the end, she came to voice her concern with her usual question.

"Was it really worth it?"

She started asking me that question half-way through the season and I always had a retort ready.

"They have expectations."

"And who is they?"

I hesitated. "The team. The players. The fans."

"Wrong," she observed. "It's you. You're the one putting these demands on yourself. Players and fans wouldn't think anything of it if someone else was wearing that suit."

"I can't afford to lose this job, though."

"Think about it," Emmy said. "You tried to leave once and they pulled you back in. Do you really think they'd really let you go?"

She had a point. My fears of being fired were likely overexaggerated. Rick had said it himself in the beer cooler during my first season—people weren't exactly lining up for a chance at this job. And when I did try to leave before, he was on the phone with me the following spring, searching for some way to pull me back in.

"You could just do the minimum, and they'd keep signing your checks. You don't need to kill yourself over a job like this. You have bigger things in your future."

We rehashed this conversation for months, but suddenly, something clicked. Perhaps it was just my prefrontal cortex enjoying the increased functionality that comes with age, or maybe it was the realization that this job—whatever it had become in my mind—was temporary. If I had wanted to turn it into a career, I might have been able to do that, but then why waste the time and money working toward my master's degree? Why was I going on to study writing and literature if my passion lay in costumes and sports? The answers to these questions were simple—this was not my passion. Working as a mascot was simply the most palatable job available to me while I was working my way through college. But it was also something few people got the chance to do (not that many had actually wanted to give it a try), but it still felt special. It was not a career, but neither was it "just a job" to me.

In any case, Emmy was right. It was time for me to move on to the next chapter in life, and I was finally ready to do that.

\#

Word spread fast among the booster club. Not a game or promotion would pass without someone seeking me out just to ask if the rumor was true.

"You're really leaving us?" Mrs. Drum, president of the booster club, had asked.

I had known her for most of my life. She taught first grade at Waterford Elementary—the primary school that I had attended. Her daughter, Jenny, was a year older than me and we had been friends back in high school. Later we reconnected in college, and if I had any true fans, Mrs. Drum and Jenny would have perhaps been counted among them.

"Yeah," I said. "I think it's time."

"No, C. Wolf," Jenny whined. "You can't go. It just won't be the same."

"You at least have to come and say goodbye," Mrs. Drum followed.

"There are still a few games left," I said. "I'll see you before I head to Slippery Rock."

"No," Mrs. Drum said. "To the boosters I mean. We'll be having our annual dinner in a few weeks. I think we'll have to make you the guest of honor."

As C. Wolf, I had been the guest of honor before. I had thrown out some first pitches at games, served as the grand marshal at a few local parades, appeared in some baseball documentaries, and had several spots on local media. But then again, the guest of honor wasn't me. It was C. Wolf. This was the first time anyone had invited me to be the guest of honor at anything as myself. How could I say no to something like that?

After a moment of consideration, I offered Mrs. Drum the only answer I could.

"Sure. What would you need me to do?"

"Mostly eat," Mrs. Drum said. "But maybe you could say a few words. Give us a little farewell speech."

"What would you want me to say?"

"Anything," Mrs. Drum said. "Talk about whatever you want."

***

The room was relatively small, decked out with between five and ten folding tables. When I took my seat, many of the boosters greeted me at my table. Many were still wearing their SeaWolves Boosters attire—black sweatshirts and polos. With the exception of two or three high school and college students, the group was a blend of baby boomers who were eyeing retirement and those who had slid into it long before. Emmy came along for support. We ate and chatted with everyone, and then the time came for my speech. At that moment, everything I had planned to say slipped right out of my head. Even the notes I had brought with me were suddenly garbled and unintelligible. I was used to interacting with these folks as C. Wolf, but now facing them without the mask, I was at a loss.

From what I remember, I thanked them for their support over the years. After all, it was the boosters who had transported me to PNC Park, the first Major League ballpark in which I ever performed. They had donated the props and provided key funds that enabled me to elevate my performance over the past three seasons. But as I stammered, offering up my gratitude, I felt that I was somehow letting them down. Now, writing this book, perhaps I can make it up to them, and share with them the words that seemed to evade me at the time. So here is my message for the SeaWolves Booster Club Members from 2004 to 2006—the speech I should have given then, but couldn't have written entirely without the perspective offered by the decade that would follow:

Dear Boosters:

If I were Charles Dickens, I would write about my experiences as C. Wolf in the following way:

It was the best of jobs; it was the worst of jobs; it was a dream; it was a nightmare; it was opportunity; it was adversity; but most of all, from October 2003 to September 2006, C. Wolf was me.

When Mrs. Drum asked me to speak to you, I had no idea what I would talk about. All I knew was that one of my most formative experiences—working as C. Wolf—was about to end, and I wasn't really sure how to feel about it.

Growing up, I had always struggled with a lack of confidence. I was always a smaller kid at school, thin as a snake-rail fence, and half as tall. I didn't have many friends. When I started college, many of my social issues continued. Juggling work and school schedules left little time to really connect with people in any genuine way. I seemed to develop only quirky, superficial friendships that crumbled at the first signs of any challenge. Little did I know then that all of that was about to change.

In my sophomore year at Edinboro, I accepted a unique job offer that would change my life and stepped into the role of Shooter, the mischievous mascot of the Erie Otters, and for the first time in my life people responded to me in ways that I had never experienced. I went from being overlooked—you know that short guy that people would literally not notice because they had been looking over me the entire time—to someone who, for obvious reasons, could not be missed. It may have been the mangy fur coat, the struggle with perpetual body odor, or the fact that I would randomly throw myself down the stairs for nothing but the amusement of others—but whatever the reason, people were finally paying attention to me. It was frightening, but also a little amazing.

When I was approached by the SeaWolves in October of 2003, I didn't really know what to say. I had been doing this whole mascot thing for a little over a year, but apparently, I had developed a bit of a talent for self-deprecation—and did you know that you can put a price tag on that? You can. Everyone has a price—and mine was tens of dollars—per day.

My willingness to humiliate myself was largely a part of my success as Shooter, but when I stepped into C. Wolf's shoes, I discovered that there was more to me than that. Shooter's personality was more reserved than C. Wolf's. C. Wolf was boisterous, confident. Being the only mascot in baseball who talked has that effect on you, I guess. Still, the more I worked as C. Wolf, the more our personalities became intertwined. Although there were still moments of self-deprecation, there were also moments of sheer showboating. I didn't just throw myself down the stairs anymore. That's below C. Wolf's dignity. In Double-A, I did handsprings, did stunts with hula hoops and ziplines. I've rubbed elbows with Major Leaguers like Justin Verlander, Curtis Granderson, Mike Rabelo, and Brent Gephart (the man behind the Pittsburgh Pirates' Parrot at that time). I have stolen the show in Major League ballparks and fought an epic battle with the power rangers, just to make a little kid's wish come true.

Through C. Wolf, I made new friends—real friends—and I count many of you among them. I developed confidence in myself, for the first time in my life. Being C. Wolf has fundamentally changed who I am. Because of this experience, I have found love—with Emmy—and through my continued stupidity I have come to realize just how much she cares about me. She is my constant, my rock, and my ride home from the hospital.

But now that chapter of my life is coming to an end and the path that I have walked with C. Wolf will diverge, like in Robert Frost's poem "The Road Less Traveled," only in reverse. Never fear. Though I may not be, C. Wolf will be back next year. He will still tease a smile from your lips, entice an occasional whoop. He will still exercise his stupidity for your entertainment. You will laugh, and as you do so, think of me—the ex-wolf whose exploits will linger only as distant memories. Think of me on the trail, following now a well-worn path that will lead me through graduate school and on to a promising career—whatever that career might be—and know that I will only be successful there because of my time walking the wolf's path. It was that wild journey that set me free.

Thank you for being a part of it.

Photo Gallery

Ruefman out and about as Shooter in 2002.

Ruefman dancing on dugouts in Erie & Pittsburgh in 2004.

Ruefman appearing in character at an after-game concert in 2006.

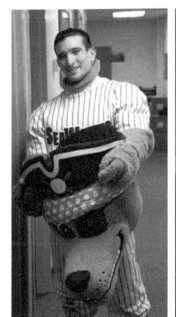

Ruefman caught with head off while on the job during the 2005 and 2006 seasons.

Acknowledgements

There are many people I have to thank for their support over the years. First, my heartfelt thanks to the front office staff of the Erie Otters (2002-2003) and SeaWolves (2003-2006), as well as their respective booster clubs. You offered me an opportunity for rare, formative experiences, without which I would not be who I am today.

To my critique partners, Jeremiah Bass, Andy Cochran, and Kevin Drzakowski. Your suggestions and advice over the years not only made this a better book, but they have made me a better writer.

My gratitude also goes out to my early readers and personal support group, Jonny McCalla, Kim Zagorski, and the McCulloughs (Kelly & Laura), whose early reviews of "that was funny" and "this book is entirely readable" encouraged me to retrieve this project from the proverbial trash bin and start sending it out.

To everyone at Urban Olive and Vine—particularly Carol and Chad—for the quiet window seat and countless cups of tea.

Finally, my eternal love and gratitude goes to my family—most notably to my wife and kids—who continue to humor this little "hobby" of mine. I couldn't do any of this without you.

About the Author

Daniel Ruefman writes fantasy, nonfiction, and books for younger readers. To date, he has released three collections of poetry, a children's picture book, and a memoir, *What the Fuzz? Survival Stories of a Minor League Mascot.*

In addition to his book-length works, his poetry and prose has appeared widely in literary magazines and journals including *Adelaide, Barely South Review, Burningword, FLARE: Flagler Review, SLAB (Sound and Literary Arts Book)*, and *Thin Air Magazine,* among others.

Daniel holds a Bachelor of Arts in Writing from Edinboro University of Pennsylvania, a Master of Arts in English from Slippery Rock University, and a Ph.D. in Composition & Applied Linguistics from Indiana University of Pennsylvania. When not writing, he teaches the craft as a Professor of Rhetoric & Composition at the University of Wisconsin – Stout. To learn more about Daniel and his work, please visit: www.danielruefman.com.

Made in the USA
Middletown, DE
08 January 2023

20635412R00120